BURIED ABUNDANCE

The Subconscious Protocol to Reclaim Wealth, Rewrite Identity, and Receive Without Resistance

Dominic Creed

It was never about becoming someone new. It was about removing what was never yours.

Table of Contents

Introduction

Excavating the Lie

You were never broken.
But you were taught to live as if you were.
To shrink.
To soften your hunger.
To dress your power in politeness.
To say "I'm grateful" when what you really meant was "I want more."
Somewhere along the way, you learned that wanting too much meant something was wrong with you. That overflow was dangerous. That too much attention, too much ease, too much money would make you unlovable or unsafe. So you adjusted. You became modest. Careful. Emotionally intelligent but energetically silent. You learned how to manage your desires in quiet—hoping the universe would reward your restraint.
But the universe doesn't reward smallness.
It doesn't pay you for being polite.
It mirrors your signal.
And if your signal has been wired to survival, suppression, or self-abandonment…
then no amount of visualization, journaling, or "alignment" will unlock what's already buried.
This book isn't here to teach you how to manifest.
You already know how to do that.
This book is here to **unbury** what's been rejected.
To find the original fracture—the hidden lie that told you you had to earn abundance by being good, spiritual, quiet, or healed enough.
And then dismantle it. Burn it. Rewrite it from the root.
You don't need more mindset tricks. You need a protocol that speaks the language of your nervous system, subconscious, and energetic field—*not your logical mind.*
Because that's where the block is.
And that's where we're going.

You will not find fluff here.

No high-vibe affirmations.

No false promises.

No polished lists of "5 signs you're manifesting your dreams."

Instead, what you'll find is a **subconscious protocol**—a layered system to:

- Rewire the hidden frequencies that have been repelling the very things you say you want
- Collapse the outdated identity you've been unconsciously holding onto
- Teach your body how to feel safe receiving more than it's ever held

This is not about healing every wound.

It's about building a new energetic operating system, from the inside out.

You'll be given tools. Language. Scripts. Inner codes.

But more importantly, you'll be given **permission**—not the kind that comes from someone else, but the kind that's been dormant in your cells, waiting to be triggered.

This book isn't just information. It's an invocation.

By the time you finish, you'll either be unchanged—or unrecognizable.

Because *Buried Abundance* isn't something you learn.

It's something you remember.

And once you do, the version of you that was playing small will feel like a dream you forgot to keep having.

This is your excavation.

Let's begin.

The Myth of Modesty: Why You Were Taught to Hide Your Power

From a young age, you were trained to dim yourself—not through punishment, but through praise. You were applauded for being humble, admired for being selfless, and told that asking for too much made you greedy, selfish, or ungrateful. Somewhere between the compliments and the subtle corrections, a lie took root: **that it was safer to be small.**

Modesty became a survival strategy. And you wore it well.

You learned how to take just enough, but never too much. How to work hard, but not shine too brightly. How to feel desire, but immediately shrink it behind a smile, a sigh, or a spiritual rationalization. "I don't need that." "I should just be grateful for what I have." "If it's meant for me, it'll come."

You started calling this maturity. Or grace. Or surrender. But it was never any of those things.

It was programming.

And that programming didn't just shape your mindset—it shaped your energetic field. It taught your body that **visibility was dangerous,** that **receiving was risky,** and that **being fully expressed would come at a cost.**

This isn't just cultural. It's spiritual. Many of the traditions you were drawn to in your awakening—whether they were rooted in Eastern philosophy, mystical Christianity, or the wellness movement—carried the same unspoken message: **that abundance is something you transcend, not embody.**

You were told that ego was the enemy. That wanting more meant you weren't "aligned." That needing money proved you hadn't healed your root chakra. And so, you spiritualized your silence. You made your suppression sacred.

But there is nothing holy about shrinking.

There is nothing evolved about hiding your power under the illusion of virtue.

What you've called modesty has often been fear in disguise. And what you've called humility has too often been a nervous system bracing against the consequences of being fully seen.

9

Because for many of us, being seen once meant being hurt. Being powerful once meant being punished. Wanting more once meant being labeled difficult, dramatic, or dangerous. So we learned to associate abundance with loss. Expression with rejection. Power with abandonment.

This is not a mindset issue. It's an energetic wound. And like all wounds, it doesn't dissolve through logic. It dissolves through light—the kind that doesn't just shine, but **exposes**.

So let's expose it.

Look at how easily you say "I don't need much." Look at how uncomfortable you get when someone compliments your success. Look at how quickly you rush to explain, to soften, to defer when the attention turns toward you. Look at how quickly you shrink after a breakthrough—how you unconsciously sabotage the momentum just as things start to rise.

This isn't coincidence. It's code.

You've been living under an invisible agreement: **If I stay small, I stay safe.**

But what if staying small has become the very thing that's keeping you stuck?

What if your modesty is no longer protection—but a prison?

The mind will tell you this shrinking is strategic. That if you ask for less, you'll seem more grateful. That if you shine a little less, people will love you more. That if you wait quietly, you'll be chosen. But the body knows the truth. The body knows the cost. It knows how much energy it takes to hold back what wants to rise. It knows what it feels like to constantly compress your desire, to delay your yes, to apologize for your light.

You've probably noticed it. That tension in the chest when you're about to say what you really want. The throat constriction when you're finally recognized. The sudden exhaustion after a moment of visibility or success. That's not coincidence either. It's the result of a nervous system that has learned to associate abundance with danger.

This conditioning isn't accidental. Entire systems have thrived on your silence. Economies, institutions, and even belief structures were built to benefit from your withdrawal. If you never fully claim your voice, someone else gets to speak for you. If you never take up space, someone else gets to fill it. If you never activate your power, you become easy to guide, mold, or monetize.

This is what makes the myth of modesty so seductive. It parades as virtue. It convinces you that being self-suppressing is being selfless. It teaches you to reject desire in the name of goodness. And slowly, it convinces you that less is not only enough—but somehow more noble.

But there is nothing noble about abandoning yourself.

There is nothing admirable about staying quiet when your soul is screaming. And there is nothing sacred about disconnecting from the current of abundance that wants to move through you.

You were taught to believe that power corrupts, that money tempts, that desire distracts. But the real corruption has never been in the abundance itself. It has been in the systems that made you feel guilty for wanting it.

Because when someone controls your desire, they control your decisions. They control what you allow, what you chase, what you tolerate. If you're taught that wanting is wrong, you'll stop wanting loudly. You'll start asking for permission. You'll wait to be validated instead of acting from your own knowing.

And in that space between desire and permission, your life gets outsourced. This is why modesty, when weaponized, becomes a form of control. It's not about humility. It's about hierarchy. It's about keeping you just humble enough to stay quiet, just grateful enough to not ask for more, just spiritual enough to self-sacrifice in the name of alignment.

But alignment was never meant to mean poverty. Humility was never meant to mean invisibility. Spirituality was never meant to be synonymous with struggle.

True power doesn't require explanation. It doesn't need to be justified by suffering. It doesn't ask you to choose between expansion and integrity. It invites you to remember that you were born with access, and that no system, tradition, or teacher has the right to revoke that.

The unlearning begins when you stop moralizing your limits. When you stop calling your fear wisdom. When you stop dressing your scarcity in spiritual language.

It begins when you name the truth: that you've been trained to hide, but that hiding is no longer safe.

You weren't born modest. You were trained to be.

You weren't born to dim. You were conditioned to.

The world didn't tell you to be small because it loved you. It told you to be small because you were powerful.

And now, your life will begin to shift the moment you stop apologizing for that power.

Let yourself want more. Let yourself be seen. Let yourself speak, claim, and walk in the fullness of who you are.

Because modesty was never your virtue.

It was your cage.

Abundance as Birthright, Not Reward

There is a quiet lie woven into nearly everything you've been taught about abundance:

That you must earn it.

Deserve it.

Prove yourself for it.

Work harder, be better, purify yourself more.

Only then, perhaps, abundance will come.

This is a lie so deeply embedded in your psyche that you've likely mistaken it for truth. It is reinforced by the stories you grew up hearing, by the systems you live inside, and even by the spiritual frameworks you may have turned to for liberation. The idea that abundance is a *reward*—something external, conditional, and delayed—has formed the foundation of your relationship with wealth, with opportunity, with power, and with receiving itself.

But what if that foundation is the very thing keeping you from it?

When a child is born, we don't ask what they've done to deserve breath. We don't make them prove their worthiness for nourishment, love, or safety. We understand, instinctively, that their existence alone makes them worthy of care. Their aliveness is enough.

That understanding, though, begins to erode as we grow. Somewhere along the way, worth is converted into currency. Value becomes transactional. Abundance is placed on a pedestal you can only reach through effort, self-denial, or achievement. Suddenly, you are no longer allowed to receive just because you are. You must earn your place, earn your visibility, earn your rest, earn your desires.

This isn't just conditioning. It's a form of energetic exile. You're taught that what is yours by nature must now be granted by authority. That joy, freedom, wealth, even time—are things you must win through struggle. And if you receive too easily, too quickly, or too much? You will be made to feel guilty for it. Suspicious of it. As if grace were a trick and ease were a threat. The deeper danger of this paradigm is not just in what it withholds, but in what it programs. It doesn't just keep abundance far away. It makes you feel *wrong* for expecting it.

You've been trained to believe that the more you sacrifice, the more you're owed. That pain is some kind of spiritual currency. That the universe is keeping score, and if you endure enough, it will eventually pay out.

But the universe is not a vending machine. And abundance is not a reward for how well you've played by rules that were never made for you.

Abundance is your **starting point**, not your finish line.

It is the energetic state you were designed to live from. It is not something you acquire, but something you *remember* how to hold. Like gravity, it does not need to be convinced. It simply is.

Nature does not negotiate its worth. The tree does not ask the sky if it may bloom. The ocean does not seek approval before it overflows. The sun does not dim to prove it is humble. Life, in its purest form, is unapologetically abundant. And you, whether you have realized it yet or not, are made of that same life.

But the systems around you have taught you otherwise. They have told you that if you're struggling, it's because you need to "learn a lesson." That if you're poor, it must be because of your mindset. That if you want more, you must first prove you can live with less.

This teaching is not wisdom. It is programming. It keeps you spiritually obedient and energetically disempowered. It teaches you to see abundance as something withheld—rather than something waiting.

And the moment you begin to see through this, something inside you starts to shift. Not because a secret has been revealed, but because something ancient has been remembered.

This remembering isn't intellectual. It doesn't arrive through logic or positive thinking. It arrives in your bones. In your breath. In the silence between thoughts when you stop performing for approval and let yourself exist, fully and unapologetically.

And in that stillness, you begin to feel it: the quiet knowing that you do not need to chase what was never lost. You were never cut off from abundance. You were taught to doubt your access to it. The disconnect isn't in the external world. It's in the internal map you've been following, one that told you to work harder, give more, expect less.

Unlearning that map takes more than affirmation. It takes dismantling an entire worldview that measured your worth in productivity, humility, and self-denial. It takes stepping out of the performance of virtue and into the unapologetic act of receiving. Not from greed. Not from entitlement. But from truth. From alignment with what's always been yours.

Receiving becomes sacred when it's no longer conditional. When it's no longer earned through self-sacrifice or delayed until someone else decides you're ready. It becomes a natural extension of who you are. Just like exhaling follows inhaling, receiving follows being. Not because you proved yourself, but because you remembered yourself.

This doesn't mean abundance looks the same for everyone. It doesn't mean it will show up in the exact form you expect. But it does mean you are always in relationship with it. You are either allowing it or blocking it. You are either opening to it or arguing with it. And those patterns are often invisible until they're named.

Some block it with shame: "Who am I to have more than others?"

Some with guilt: "I should just be grateful for what I have."

Others with fear: "If I receive too much, I'll lose it. Or I'll be judged. Or something bad will happen."

These are not signs of spiritual maturity. They are symptoms of spiritual distortion. Abundance does not require you to abandon empathy or humility. But it does ask you to stop performing smallness as a virtue. It asks you to stop using lack as your identity badge. It asks you to stop proving your goodness through suffering.

You cannot access true abundance while still apologizing for wanting it.

There's a reason the energy of abundance is often associated with the feminine: not because it belongs to women, but because it follows the same principles as feminine receptivity. It does not respond to force. It opens in the presence of surrender. It flows where there is space, not pressure. It nourishes, but only when welcomed.

This energy has been buried in you—not lost, but hidden beneath years of conditioning. And when you begin to excavate it, you may notice resistance. You may feel unworthy. You may want to turn back. That's the old map trying to reroute you to a destination you no longer desire. You don't need it anymore.

The new map isn't written in steps or strategies. It's felt in the body. It's lived in the way you hold yourself, the way you speak your truth, the way you stop justifying your needs and start honoring them. It's built on an internal knowing that says, without needing to shout it: "I belong to abundance. Not because I earned it. But because I am it."

This shift changes everything. It doesn't just change your relationship to money. It changes how you walk into a room. How you show up to conversations. How you price your work, speak your needs, accept compliments, rest without guilt, and say no without apology.

Abundance stops being a thing you chase and starts becoming a frequency you emit. And the more you embody it, the more the world rearranges to match it. Not as a reward, but as a mirror.

When you stop trying to become worthy, you remember that you already are.

And from that place, receiving becomes inevitable.

This Is Not a Book. It's an Excavation

If you picked up this book expecting another list of steps, another positive thinking formula, another shiny trick for manifesting more—pause now. This is not that.

This is not a motivational text dressed in spiritual language. This is not a how-to for hustling in prettier clothes. This is not another prescription to upgrade your mindset while leaving the root untouched. This is not a self-help manual at all.

This is an excavation.

What you are holding in your hands is a living architecture. A coded transmission designed to break apart the inner constructs that have buried your abundance beneath years of programming, performance, and spiritual distortion. It is not here to teach you something new. It is here to unearth what was always inside you—what was buried, hidden, or made unacceptable by the systems you were born into.

This book will not simply *tell* you how to access wealth. It will *deactivate* the lies that told you it wasn't already yours.

The work ahead is not light, but it is sacred. Each chapter is not information. It is invocation. Each paragraph is a pressure point designed to disrupt the narrative that has kept you small. If you let it, this book will not just change your thoughts. It will change your field. It will interrupt the silent agreements you've made with scarcity, guilt, and fear, and invite you to walk a different path.

Not as a seeker.

As a sovereign.

If that feels too big, too much, too soon—good. That discomfort is not a sign of misalignment. It's a sign that you're touching something true. Most people don't reject abundance because they don't want it. They reject it because they don't know how to hold it without collapsing the identity that made them lovable, safe, or spiritually accepted.

Abundance is not hard to manifest. It's hard to allow.

It threatens the masks you've worn. It confronts the beliefs you've used to survive. It asks you to stop pretending you're still waiting for permission.

That's what this excavation is about. Not just digging up your desires. Digging up the structures that said those desires were dangerous. Digging up the voices that told you receiving made you selfish. Digging up the

17

theology that said suffering was holy. Digging up the trauma that taught you to fear overflow. Digging up the internal systems that keep rebuilding lack no matter how much you try to escape it.

That's why this book is not a casual read. It is an activation. A ritual. A rewiring process. The words on these pages are not just meant to be understood. They are meant to be *received* in the body, in the breath, in the energy field. You are not here to study the book. You are here to *let the book study you*—to find the parts that flinch when abundance is mentioned, to surface the agreements you made with powerlessness, and to walk you, piece by piece, back to yourself.

This is a remembering.

A collapse.

A reconfiguration.

And it's not something you do once and then move on. Excavation is a rhythm. A return. A deepening. As you move through these chapters, you may feel resistance. You may feel grief. You may feel old identities start to crack. That is the point.

You are not here to become more.

You are here to unbury what already was.

The discomfort you might feel as you read is not a sign that something's wrong. It's a signal that something long buried is surfacing. The system you've built inside—the one that trades safety for suppression, that confuses goodness with invisibility—was constructed to protect you from pain. But that same system now prevents you from receiving.

So much of what you've internalized as "spiritual" has in fact been control. So much of what you've called "humble" was learned survival. You were taught to see your bigness as arrogance, your visibility as vanity, your overflow as excess. And now, even as you try to grow, to open, to expand, there's a reflex inside you that still equates power with danger.

This book will keep pressing on that reflex.

It will ask you to question the holiness of sacrifice. To see where you were praised for your emptiness. To notice where you were loved for needing nothing. It will ask you to notice how often your "gratitude" was a cover for fear. How often your "modesty" was a disguise for shame. And how many times you said no to more—not because you didn't want it, but because some old part of you believed that having more meant being less lovable, less pure, less safe.

We are not here to glorify lack. We are not here to decorate it with pretty affirmations and hope it hurts less. We are here to dismantle it at the root. And to do that, you must become honest.

Honest about what you want.

Honest about what you've feared.

Honest about who you've been trained to become.

The work ahead is not linear. There is no ten-step map to becoming a receiver. What you will find instead are patterns to dissolve, rituals to reclaim, frequencies to tune into, and a deep, sacred confrontation with the parts of you that still whisper, "It's not safe to have it all."

Those whispers may be ancestral. They may be cultural. They may have been etched into you by religion, by gender, by trauma, by survival. This book will not argue with those voices. It will hold them to the light. And then it will offer you the tools to choose differently.

You are not here to be reformed.

You are here to be returned to.

Every word that follows is encoded with this intention. Not to instruct. To awaken. Not to teach. To remind. Not to fix. To reveal.

You don't need to become worthy. You already are.

You don't need to be more spiritual. You already are.

You don't need to prove you're ready. You already are.

All that's left is to clear the debris.

To unlearn the loyalty to smallness.

To break the agreement with quiet suffering.

To dissolve the scaffolding around your light.

This is not a book for passivity. It is for participation. If you move through these pages with only your mind, you'll understand. But if you move through them with your field, your breath, your body—you'll transform. You'll feel old reflexes loosen. You'll notice where your energy contracts, where your throat tightens, where your nervous system clings to struggle like an identity.

And in those moments, you will have a choice.

Not to go back.

But to go deeper.

Into the place beneath the programming.
Into the part of you that always knew.
Into the buried abundance that was never lost—only hidden.
This is the excavation. And it begins now.

Part I. Rewiring the Hidden Patterns

You were never blocked by money.

You were blocked by the programs that taught you what to expect, what to tolerate, and what to feel guilty for wanting.

These next chapters are not about teaching you how to *get* abundance. They are about removing the blindfold that made you forget you were already woven from it.

If you've tried manifestation methods, wealth books, or mindset hacks before and still found yourself stuck in cycles—this is the part that explains why. Because no technique can override the frequency of your core identity. And identity is shaped not by logic, but by what you've been trained to feel safe around.

Safety, in many of us, is fused with smallness. With waiting. With being grateful for crumbs and ashamed of desire. With calling yourself humble while quietly choking on everything you've swallowed just to be accepted.

This part of the book goes underneath that wiring.

We start by revealing the hidden codes that govern your ability to receive— things like permission, identity, and historical suppression. You'll see how much of your life has been lived from inherited beliefs, subconscious defenses, and emotional reflexes that were installed long before you were aware.

You were not born ashamed of wanting more.

You were not born afraid of being seen.

You were not born to beg the world for what already lives in your field.

But the programming has been consistent. Cultural, spiritual, generational. Many of us were conditioned to associate goodness with sacrifice, purity with struggle, and virtue with invisibility. And because those messages were repeated through praise, religion, parenting, school, and social dynamics, they embedded themselves not just in your mind—but in your nervous system.

So now, even when you say you want more, there is a part of you that flinches.

You might notice it when money starts to flow, and guilt kicks in.

When someone praises your power, and you deflect it.

When you're about to invest in yourself, and your chest tightens.

That flinch is the frequency we're here to rewire.

Not by force.

Not by bypassing pain.

But by reclaiming the truth that was buried beneath the programming.

Part I is about decoding those hidden truths.

It's about understanding why you were taught to wait, why deserving doesn't equal receiving, and why your struggle was never a sign of lack—but of distortion.

We will work with energy.

With language.

With memory.

With cellular reflex.

Because transformation doesn't come from knowing more. It comes from feeling something real enough to undo what you were taught to believe.

Let yourself move slowly through what's ahead. Not intellectually, but viscerally. Track where your body tenses, where your field constricts, where your mind rushes to justify the old identity.

Every flinch is a doorway.

Every discomfort is an invitation.

And every truth you reclaim brings you one layer closer to the natural receiver you were always meant to be.

The rewiring begins here.

Chapter 1. The Buried Codes of Receiving

The Energy of Deserving vs. the Frequency of Permission

Many people spend years trying to feel more *worthy*. They repeat affirmations, attend workshops, and write in journals: *I am enough. I deserve good things. I am worthy of abundance.* And yet, nothing seems to shift.

This is the trap of the "worthiness" loop.

It sounds empowering, but it quietly reinforces the idea that there's still something you must *convince yourself* of before you can receive. It implies that once you finally *feel* worthy enough, the door to abundance will swing open. But worthiness is not the problem. It never was.

You are already worthy.

You always were.

Even when you were broke, messy, confused, ashamed, lost, angry, disconnected, or self-destructive. None of those things ever made you unworthy. They only made you human.

The real blockage is not about deserving.

It's about *permission.*

Deserving is passive. It's about being "good enough" in someone else's eyes. It waits. It hopes. It seeks validation.

Permission is active. It's an internal command. It does not beg. It does not need approval. It simply chooses. Energetically, it says: *This is mine. I choose to hold it. I am ready to receive it now.*

Most people who feel stuck in their manifestation journey are not struggling with unworthiness. They're struggling with unclaimed permission. They believe they need to earn abundance—through performance, proof, or perfection. And this keeps them locked in a frequency of striving, which repels the very thing they desire.

Because the field responds not to effort, but to energetic certainty.

You can do all the work to "feel worthy" and still secretly hold a deep resistance to receiving. That resistance often sounds like:

- *What if it's too much?*
- *What will people think if I suddenly succeed?*
- *Will I still be loved if I stop struggling?*

- *Do I really know what to do with this power?*

These questions don't come from a lack of worthiness. They come from the subconscious belief that it's not *safe* or *allowed* to fully step into your abundance.

Permission is what turns a desire into a reality. It is the energetic "yes" beneath your words, your posture, your presence. You don't wait for someone to give it to you. You give it to yourself.

In fact, the entire system you're learning in this book is built around reclaiming permission at deeper and deeper levels. Not the kind of permission that comes from rebellious declarations or spiritual bypassing—but the kind that radiates from a stable, embodied knowing:

I am allowed to want what I want.

I am allowed to have it.

I am allowed to hold it.

I am allowed to enjoy it without guilt.

You may intellectually agree with those statements. But agreeing is not the same as embodying. The nervous system often tells the truth faster than the mind. So here's a way to test this for yourself.

Think of an amount of money, love, attention, or visibility that you deeply desire. Hold that image in your mind. Now ask yourself: *Do I feel totally calm and grounded with the idea of receiving that much? Or does something tighten in me?*

That tightening is the edge between deserving and permission.

It reveals where you still subconsciously associate more with danger. And until that association is rewired, you'll keep subconsciously pushing it away—even as you affirm your worthiness aloud.

That tightening in the body, that subtle contraction, is not random. It's a form of unspoken loyalty—to your past, your lineage, your conditioning. It says, "I can't go beyond what I've seen. I can't allow more than what was modeled for me." This is why so many people can dream vividly, speak positively, and visualize constantly, but still hit the same invisible ceiling. Energetically, they're saying: "I want more... but I haven't made it safe to have more."

Permission is not granted by mantras or intention alone. It is anchored through internal authority. That means choosing yourself when no one else does. That means receiving without explanation. That means allowing beauty, money, love, and pleasure to exist in your life without attaching shame to it.

The collective is deeply conditioned to idolize struggle. Especially those raised in spiritual, religious, or culturally modest environments. You were taught that excess is indulgence, that ease is laziness, that wealth is dangerous unless hard-earned. And so, even after doing the "inner work," there's a tendency to hesitate when life begins to offer more.

What you are really being asked to do is stop seeking permission from the external world. The system you were born into benefits from your hesitation. It thrives when you delay. It rewards your overexertion, your guilt, your need to justify success. It teaches you to play small and praise yourself for being humble.

But the frequency of permission feels like unbothered knowing. Not arrogance, not superiority—simply a settled truth within. It says: "I don't need to explain why I have this. I don't need to apologize for holding this. I don't need to wait until others catch up. I am allowed, now."

This shift in frequency is subtle but absolute. And it's this shift that flips the field around you.

Because the universe doesn't just listen to your words—it listens to your self-concept. And your self-concept is not built through worthiness rituals alone. It is built through repeated acts of permission. Small moments when you say yes to the thing you thought you needed to earn. When you take the seat, wear the dress, name the price, close the deal, open the account, receive the love, post the truth, hold the gaze—before you feel fully ready.

That is when the permission field expands.

Not when the external finally confirms your worth. But when your nervous system feels you choose yourself, and learns that it's safe to do so.

What you permit is what you receive. Not what you beg for. Not what you hope for. What you energetically stand for.

And standing for something is not about becoming louder. It's about becoming cleaner in your energy. No more mixed signals. No more inner contradictions between what you say you want and what you secretly resist. This subchapter is not asking you to chase abundance more forcefully. It's inviting you to locate and remove the subtle inner brakes that keep your power suppressed. Because the more you cling to proving worthiness, the more you affirm that something is still missing.

25

You don't need to prove. You need to permit.

There is a you that exists beyond the emotional debt of your upbringing. A version of you that does not ask if it's too much, too soon, too bold. That version already lives within you. But it will not emerge until you allow it. Not when you finish healing. Not when you're less afraid. Not when you're more perfect.

Now.

The field responds to your internal green light. Every time.

Why the Feminine Was Taught to Wait

There's a quiet programming that lives in the cells of those who carry the feminine. It says: wait your turn. Don't take too much. Be good. Be grateful. Be patient. Let others go first.

This conditioning doesn't arrive all at once. It's layered over lifetimes, religions, stories, laws, wounds. It's the unspoken inheritance passed through glances, silences, subtle corrections. And it rarely names itself. Instead, it hides inside praise: "She's so selfless." "She never complains." "She's strong—she always makes do with so little."

At the root of this programming is a deep, generational distortion: that the feminine must earn her place through endurance. That her worth is proven by what she can tolerate. That receiving is something she must wait for—never something she can claim outright.

Historically, systems were built to keep her in that waiting room. Inheritance laws were written to favor the masculine. Religious doctrines cast the feminine as temptress, distraction, lesser vessel. Women were barred from owning property, managing wealth, holding power in courts, councils, and temples. Their access to resources was filtered through fathers, husbands, and priests.

And when material wealth was inaccessible, spiritual teachings filled the gap. She was told that her virtue lay in modesty, her power in sacrifice. That desire was dangerous. That ambition was masculine. That humility was holy. Over time, she internalized these codes. Not just intellectually, but somatically. The body itself began to brace. To shrink. To apologize.

But this isn't just history—it's energy. The conditioning of the feminine is not merely a social phenomenon. It's an energetic imprint, passed down and reinforced through generations of survival, suppression, and shame.

Even today, the modern feminine is often caught in the echo of this dynamic. She's praised for being "low maintenance," for not needing much. She's admired for her resilience, her ability to give endlessly without asking in return. But beneath that praise is a hidden cost: the suppression of her natural receptivity.

The feminine is not passive. She is receptive. That's not weakness—it's power. True receiving is not waiting. It is magnetism, spaciousness, sovereignty. It is the knowing that abundance is her native state, not something she must chase, earn, or be granted by someone else.

But when that knowing is buried, a different pattern emerges. She begins to seek validation before receiving. She waits to be chosen. She delays her desires until others are satisfied. She suppresses her hunger so as not to offend. She interprets her own expansion as danger, threat, or selfishness.

And so, even in a modern world where opportunity appears more available, many who embody the feminine still hesitate at the threshold of abundance. They still ask for permission with their energy. They still tone themselves down, hold themselves back, overgive in hopes of eventually being allowed to receive.

This isn't personal failure. It's inherited programming.

And the danger of this programming is that it often masquerades as maturity, patience, or grace. But if you look closely, you'll find that much of what has been praised as "grace" in the feminine is actually quiet resignation. A kind of soul-level fatigue from centuries of being last in line.

This book is not interested in continuing that line.

It's not here to affirm your worth. You already know you are worthy. It's here to unearth the subconscious contracts that say: "Even in my worthiness, I must wait."

Because until those are broken, you will keep circling the same pattern. Saying the right affirmations. Doing the inner work. Visualizing your desires. But always keeping them at arm's length. Not because you don't believe you deserve them—but because you were taught, energetically, that receiving too quickly, too easily, too fully… is dangerous.

You don't need more permission slips from culture, from spirituality, or even from healing. You need the memory of what was stolen before you even knew it was yours.

The feminine was not built to wait. She was built to hold, to open, to generate, to pull life toward her with the gravity of her presence. And yet, for so long, this power has been buried beneath spiritualized scarcity. Wrapped in language that sounds holy, but keeps her small.

She is told that desire must be surrendered. That asking is ego. That ambition is misaligned. She is encouraged to release, but not to claim. To forgive, but not to take up space. To be in flow, but never to direct the current.

This creates a split. A hunger she can't name. A quiet resentment that bubbles under her surface, then turns inward. She doubts herself. Feels too much. Not enough. Too fast. Not ready. Always measuring her pace against some invisible rulebook of when and how much she's "allowed" to have.

Energetically, this plays out as tension between expansion and collapse. She opens to possibility, then quickly contracts. She visualizes what she wants, then apologizes with her actions. She becomes magnetic, then punishes herself for being seen.

All of it is part of the spell. A long-cast hypnosis that says the feminine must not move too boldly, or too soon. That her value lies in her ability to hold space for others, even at the cost of herself.

But here's the deeper truth: the feminine doesn't need to be chosen. She already is. She doesn't need to wait to receive. She is the field from which receiving is born.

This is not about gender. It is about energy. Anyone who holds the feminine frequency—no matter their body, identity, or path—knows this tension. The pressure to soften just enough to be palatable, but not so much that they disappear. The dance of making others comfortable while trying to grow. The internalized belief that stillness equals stagnation, and that power must always come through effort.

What if the waiting is the lie?

What if every moment you've spent questioning your readiness, every delay you've justified as "alignment," every time you've told yourself "not yet" was never your voice to begin with?

The feminine is not late. She is not behind. She is not unworthy, unready, or unproven. She is simply carrying the weight of lineages who were told to wait until someone else said it was time.

There is no permission slip coming. There is no gatekeeper to impress. No cosmic checklist to complete before you are allowed to expand.

The act of claiming without justification is the rebellion. The act of receiving without shrinking is the ritual.

Every time you say yes to your own fullness without preface or apology, you rupture a centuries-old pattern. You recalibrate your field to expect rather than request. To own rather than earn. To embody rather than explain.

This is not about arrogance. It is about authority. Quiet, rooted, unshakable authority that does not ask for validation. That does not shrink to fit inside palatable archetypes. That does not disguise desire as something to be healed.

The feminine doesn't need to be healed to receive. She needs to remember. And remembering means breaking the trance of waiting. It means acting in alignment with the truth that abundance is not granted—it is mirrored. Reality responds to the field you hold, not the timeline you wait for.

So if you've been waiting… waiting to feel ready, to be more healed, to prove yourself, to be less much or more deserving… ask who you're waiting for.

And then stop.

Receive now. Before it's safe. Before it's validated. Before it's perfect.

That is how you break the inheritance.

That is how you reclaim the original blueprint: the one where the feminine didn't wait to be chosen.

She chose herself. And the world bent around her choice.

The Hidden Cost of Modesty, Gratitude, and Guilt

You've likely been praised for being modest. For not asking for too much. For being grateful even when what you received wasn't enough. You were taught that these traits made you good. Humble. Spiritual. Deserving.

But no one told you that these same traits can quietly sabotage your ability to receive.

Modesty, when rooted in self-compression, becomes self-erasure. Gratitude, when used to override unmet needs, becomes a muzzle. Guilt, when left unchecked, becomes a chain that keeps abundance out of reach even when it's right in front of you.

These are not virtues in the context of your receiving field. They are distortions that feel noble while they quietly cap your expansion.

If you've ever felt uncomfortable being celebrated, uneasy asking for what you want, or ashamed of having more than others, you're not broken. You've simply absorbed emotional patterns that were never meant to be yours.

And to release them, you don't need more information. You need integration.

Integration means meeting the parts of yourself that are still carrying the emotional residue of the old rules. It means facing the fear that says, "If I stop being modest, they won't love me." The guilt that whispers, "If I have more, someone else will have less." The false virtue that says, "If I'm already blessed, I shouldn't ask for more."

None of these are yours.

But they live in your nervous system. In your breath. In the way you hesitate before saying yes to something big.

This is not about healing everything all at once. It's about creating a moment—right now—where you become aware of what you're still carrying, and begin to release it.

To do this, you will not think your way through it. You will feel. You will listen. You will speak out loud what has been hidden in silence.

Let this be a soft, slow ritual. One that you do not rush. One that you allow to unfold in your body, not just your mind.

Emotional Integration Practice: Releasing the Cost of Staying Small

Find a space where you can be undisturbed for a few minutes. Sit comfortably, with your feet on the ground or your body fully supported. This is not a performance. It is an unraveling.

Close your eyes. Begin by noticing your breath. Not changing it, just witnessing. Let your attention drop from your mind into your chest. Into your belly. Into your body.

Now bring to mind a moment in your life when you felt you had to be modest. A time you dimmed your joy, softened your voice, minimized your success, or made yourself smaller so that others would feel comfortable.

See it. Let it rise. Do not judge it. Let yourself witness who you were in that moment.

Now feel into the emotional charge of it. Is there shame? Sadness? Resentment? Regret? Let the emotions come. Stay with them.

Now speak, either out loud or in a whisper, the words you never said in that moment.

Let them come through you.

"I didn't want to make you uncomfortable, but I was proud of myself."

"I needed more than what you gave me, and I was afraid to ask."

"I made myself small because I thought it was the only way to be loved."

Let it be messy. Let it be honest. There is no wrong way to do this.

You are not reliving the moment. You are retrieving the power that got frozen there. You are updating your nervous system by allowing it to feel what it wasn't allowed to feel before.

Stay with the sensations in your body. If tears come, let them. If your body wants to move, let it. This is your release. This is your realignment.

Now, let your body soften. Let your breath deepen. Gently bring your attention to your heart. Place your hands there if it helps you feel the contact. You are safe. You are seen. You are not wrong for wanting more.

Begin to call in the version of you who never apologized for her radiance. The version of you who walked into rooms and didn't shrink. The version who knew that her receiving helped everyone, not just herself.

Feel her presence in the room. Not in a fantasy way, but as a frequency already alive in your field. You've had flashes of her before. Now let her become more clear.

Let yourself feel the words:

"My abundance does not take from anyone. My joy does not harm anyone. My having does not cause others to go without."

Say them. Whisper them if you need to. Speak them until something in your body starts to believe.

Notice if there is resistance. Maybe a part of you still clings to guilt. That's okay. Guilt is just a signal. It's not the truth. Let it show itself, and then meet it with new information.

Guilt often arises when your nervous system is carrying the energy of inherited rules. Rules like: *You should be grateful with what you have. You shouldn't ask for more. You'll make others feel bad if you succeed. Be careful not to seem greedy. Don't be too much.*

These rules were taught, modeled, praised, reinforced. But they are not laws. They are not spiritual. They are not divine.

The more you repeat your truth out loud, the more your system begins to replace those rules with new ones. Truth-based ones. Freedom-based ones. Energetically aligned ones.

Feel what it would be like to walk through the world holding this new frequency:

"It is safe for me to receive. It is holy for me to expand. It is generous for me to thrive."

This is not affirmation. This is frequency reprogramming.

Notice how your body responds when you try those words. Do they feel foreign? Do they stir something real? Let that be your signal of what still wants to be held, and what's ready to be released.

If shame arises as you do this work, do not fight it. Shame loses power in the presence of truth. You are not clearing shame by denying it. You are clearing shame by meeting it with reality.

And the reality is this: your modesty did not protect you. It protected others from having to grow. It protected the system from being disrupted. It protected the illusion that staying small is the noble path.

But you are not here to be small. You are not here to pay for someone else's comfort with your own suppression.

Now that you've felt and voiced the truth, close this ritual gently.

Place your hands on your body. Thank yourself for being brave enough to feel. To remember. To reclaim.

There is no perfect version of you waiting at the end of this journey. There is only the one who stopped making herself wait.

And from this space, receiving becomes natural again. Not because you forced it, but because you stopped blocking it with false virtue.

Let that be the real integration. You don't need to be less. You don't need to earn. You don't need to apologize for your desires.

You just need to keep remembering that it was never your job to stay small so others could stay comfortable.

Your expansion is not dangerous. Your receiving is not selfish. Your abundance is not shameful.

It's your return.

And now, something new begins.

Chapter 2. The Energetic Laws You Were Never Taught

The Law of Suppressed Abundance

There is a silent law that governs the experience of lack in this world. It doesn't appear in economics textbooks. It isn't taught in schools. It has no official name on record. But it operates with ruthless precision in the background of your life, shaping what you think you can have, what you allow yourself to want, and what you believe is appropriate to receive.

Let's call it the Law of Suppressed Abundance.

This law does not say abundance is unavailable. It doesn't even say you are unworthy of it. What it does is much more subtle and far more dangerous. It convinces you to suppress your own abundance potential by masking it beneath layers of identity, programming, and inherited beliefs.

To understand how this works, imagine abundance as a current of water flowing beneath the surface of a field. The water is always there, running just beneath your feet. It is clean, rich, potent. But you were handed a manual that told you never to dig. You were told that water like that only belongs to others. That to ask for it would make you selfish, or worse, unsafe.

So instead of tapping into the underground stream, you learned to survive on raindrops. You celebrated small trickles. You trained yourself to wait for moments of grace that came unpredictably. You might have even built a belief system around the nobility of enduring droughts.

And every time you got a glimpse of that deeper well—an intuitive knowing, a flush of desire, a sense that more was possible—something shut it down. You hesitated. You questioned. You feared what accessing that kind of power might mean about you.

This is not an accident. It's not personal failure. It's a structural pattern that has been enforced over generations. The Law of Suppressed Abundance was built into society not to protect you, but to manage you.

Because a person who believes their abundance must be earned, delayed, or spiritualized into some unreachable purity is easier to control. They won't challenge systems. They won't question limits. They will keep themselves in check out of fear of being "too much," "too greedy," or "too full of themselves."

And yet, nothing in nature agrees with this law.

The tree does not negotiate with the sky before it grows taller. The ocean does not apologize for taking up space. The sun does not ask for permission to shine a little brighter today. In fact, nature thrives not by holding back, but by expanding into its full expression—unapologetically, relentlessly, effortlessly.

You were born into that same rhythm. The suppression you feel now is not natural. It is learned.

The metaphor of buried water is not just poetic. Energetically, your system has internal reservoirs that remain untapped because your identity was shaped around containment. That containment became a form of safety. Abundance felt dangerous, not because it is, but because you were trained to believe it would destabilize your relationships, your worth, or your belonging.

At its core, the Law of Suppressed Abundance functions like a thermostat. No matter how much abundance tries to pour in from the outside—through opportunity, inspiration, love, or resources—your internal setting will reject it unless it matches what you've been conditioned to feel is "appropriate." If too much starts to come in, you unconsciously sabotage, delay, shrink, or deflect.

This is not about deserving. It's about identity regulation. If your system is wired to associate abundance with threat, betrayal, or arrogance, it will reject abundance in order to preserve your self-image and social safety.

What makes this law so effective is that it hides in virtue. It disguises itself as humility, spiritual purity, generosity, discipline. But underneath, it's the same mechanism: a learned resistance to expansion.

And unless you recognize it, you will keep mistaking suppression for alignment. You'll keep thinking you're just not ready, or not worthy, or not clear enough—when in reality, you've simply never been taught how to let abundance feel safe in your system.

If suppression is identity protection, then healing requires identity expansion. You do not break the Law of Suppressed Abundance by force or logic. You dissolve it by unlearning the false sense of safety it provides.

This begins with noticing the moments where your body says no, even when your mind says yes. That tiny contraction when someone offers you money. The awkwardness when you're celebrated. The guilt when life feels too good too fast. These are the fingerprints of suppression—unconscious flinches that protect an outdated self-image.

That self-image was shaped by the environments you came from. Maybe you were raised to believe that good people don't talk about money. Maybe you saw wealth used as a weapon, and vowed never to become "one of them." Maybe every time you succeeded, someone you loved felt smaller, and you learned to dim yourself to preserve closeness.

Suppression is not always loud. Often, it's gentle. It shows up as procrastination. Over-giving. Shrinking. Avoiding visibility. Delaying the moment where you actually allow yourself to want what you want fully. And every time that inner volume is turned down, the world mirrors it. Not because the world is withholding from you, but because it reflects the level of permission you've given yourself to receive.

This is the law in motion: abundance is never fully gone, just diverted. Energy that wants to become wealth, love, recognition, or support is quietly rerouted into safer channels. It becomes spiritual bypassing. Perfectionism. Martyrdom. You think you're waiting for the right time, but the right time never comes because the setting inside hasn't changed.

Think of your subconscious as a gatekeeper. It will not allow in what it believes might compromise your survival. If abundance feels like exposure, conflict, loss, or disconnection, the gate stays closed. And no amount of manifesting, vision boarding, or working harder will override that protective lock.

But this gate isn't sealed shut. It's attuned to emotional memory. When you begin to rewire what abundance means to your nervous system, you slowly create space for the gate to open. Not through force, but through safety.

This safety doesn't come from numbers in your bank account. It comes from the parts of you that finally believe they are allowed to expand without punishment. That expansion doesn't require betrayal, abandonment, or rejection. That being more doesn't make you less loved.

Every law has a loophole. For the Law of Suppressed Abundance, the loophole is reclamation. The moment you realize you don't need to earn abundance, justify it, or suffer for it, you become dangerous to systems that relied on your self-restriction. You step outside the script.

Reclamation is not just a mindset shift. It is a cellular remembering. A return to a deeper truth that was never erased—just buried. You begin to feel the abundance not as a future goal, but as a current that already exists. One you're finally willing to touch.

This is the difference between pursuing and receiving. Pursuit keeps you chasing what you already have, believing it's somewhere else. Receiving is the moment you stop running and turn inward, where all the suppressed energy has been waiting.

There is nothing humble about staying small. There is nothing noble about rejecting support. There is nothing enlightened about living in lack. These are not signs of spiritual maturity. They are signs of an old law running quietly beneath the surface of your life.

And the moment you name it, you weaken it.

You are not here to suppress. You are here to express. To let the energy of abundance move through you without guilt, without apology, without delay. Not because you earned it. Not because you're better than anyone else. But because it's who you are underneath all the training.

The law was never real. But your permission is. And the moment you choose it, you begin to write new laws—ones that no longer require you to shrink in order to survive.

Why "Alignment" Alone Is Not Enough

The word "alignment" has become a golden ticket in the world of manifestation. It's whispered in spiritual circles, printed on vision boards, and offered as the answer to every problem: if you were aligned, it would flow. If you were aligned, it would be easy. If you were aligned, you'd already have it.

But what if that's not entirely true?

Not because alignment doesn't matter—it does—but because the version of alignment being sold is a watered-down imitation of a much deeper truth. And chasing that imitation keeps you in the same loop, feeling like you're always *almost there*, but never quite arriving.

The current narrative around alignment is often oversimplified: feel good, think positive, act as if. And while there's truth in raising your emotional frequency and shifting your state, this version bypasses the real work. It ignores the shadows, the contractions, the body's stored trauma, and the unconscious identity structures that actually *govern* your frequency beneath the surface.

So when people say "just get into alignment," what they often mean is "just feel better." But feeling better isn't the same as rewiring your energetic architecture. Feeling better for a few minutes while still holding the internal belief that you're not safe to receive, or that too much abundance will make you a target, doesn't shift the signal you're sending. It only masks it.

This is why so many people who genuinely believe in the Law of Attraction still feel stuck. They're visualizing, scripting, meditating—but their body doesn't trust what they're calling in. Their subconscious is still holding onto the old survival patterns. And that subconscious always wins.

Because alignment is not a mood. It's not a playlist. It's not a morning routine. It's a *state of full coherence between identity, energy, action, and embodiment*. And achieving that coherence requires more than good vibes.

It requires excavation.

Real alignment isn't about faking confidence. It's about becoming congruent with the version of yourself who already has what you want—and clearing out everything within you that contradicts it.

If you desire to receive more money, but deep inside you believe that receiving will cause disconnection, jealousy, or responsibility you don't want to carry, then your energy will stay split. You'll be in "alignment" only on the surface, while the deeper current of your being is still in resistance. The universe doesn't respond to your words. It responds to your coherence.

This is where most teachings go silent. Because it's easier to sell a shortcut than to guide someone into their own nervous system and ask: *What part of you still believes abundance is dangerous?*

This is the core reason alignment alone isn't enough. If alignment doesn't include integration of the unconscious, it's not alignment—it's performance. You might momentarily convince your mind, but your body will always tell the truth.

The body is where real alignment lives.

This is why two people can say the same affirmation, but only one sees results. It's not because one is trying harder. It's because one of them *is* the affirmation, and the other is repeating words they haven't yet fully embodied. The universe doesn't reward effort. It reflects embodiment.

And embodiment only happens when there is safety in receiving. Safety in expansion. Safety in becoming the version of you who no longer uses chaos, doubt, or delay as a form of control.

True alignment is the byproduct of inner reconciliation. Of no longer sending mixed signals to life. It's the point where your thoughts, desires, expectations, and nervous system are finally speaking the same language.

That's not a mindset hack. That's energetic truth.

And here's the part most teachings miss: when you're truly aligned—not pretending, not pushing, not hoping, but actually *clear*—there is no longer tension between your desire and your reality. You stop oscillating between wanting and fearing. You stop leaking energy trying to override your inner "no" with forced affirmations. The gap collapses, not because you manipulated the external, but because you removed the internal static.

This is the real work.

It's not always glamorous. It rarely looks like a perfect morning ritual or a curated journaling session. Sometimes it looks like sitting in the discomfort of a belief you inherited from someone who was just trying to keep you safe. Sometimes it means facing the version of you that still equates visibility with danger or success with betrayal. Sometimes it's not about "doing" anything, but about letting your body finally feel what it was never allowed to feel.

That's how your energy becomes trustworthy. Not through control, but through honesty.

40

Because as long as your alignment depends on external conditions—how others perceive you, what your bank account says, whether or not your day goes smoothly—it's not alignment. It's dependency dressed in spiritual language. And that keeps you bound.

True alignment is the frequency of *nothing left to prove*.

It's quiet. It's calm. It's deep. And from that depth, you make decisions differently. You no longer chase signs or test the universe. You *become* the signal.

People who embody this don't need to hustle their way into manifestations. They don't need to fixate on timelines. They don't fall into self-blame when delays happen. They understand that the frequency they hold *is* the timeline, and the timeline will bend to it—once they stop bending themselves.

This is not about perfection. It's about coherence. You don't need to be free of every doubt or fear to receive. You just need to stop being *at war* with the parts of you that are afraid. When those parts are acknowledged, held, and no longer driving your choices, your energy stops collapsing under the weight of contradiction.

This is where the magic unfolds.

Because now, when you speak a desire, it lands differently. Your field is no longer scattering that intention across timelines, survival strategies, or people-pleasing patterns. It holds it. It grounds it. And the universe responds to that kind of clarity like a tuning fork to its match.

You've probably felt this before. A moment when you *knew* something was going to happen, and it did. Not because you forced it. Not because you micromanaged every step. But because something in you had *already become it*.

That's what we're reclaiming.

Not just alignment as a concept, but alignment as a natural state of self-permission. Alignment that includes your fear and still moves forward. Alignment that honors your timing, your intuition, your integrity—not just your goals.

This is what the surface-level teachings miss. They offer tools without integration. Vision without grounding. Desire without nervous system safety. And then they leave you wondering why nothing's sticking.

But you are not here to perform worthiness. You are here to remember that receiving is your nature—not your reward.

And once you drop the script of forced alignment and step into the reality of full energetic coherence, life stops testing you and starts responding to you. Not because you earned it, but because you stopped resisting it.
That's the difference.
And it changes everything.

The Sacred Mechanics of Expansion

You were born to expand.

Not just in the spiritual sense. Not just in terms of potential or possibility. But in the very real, energetic capacity to receive. Every time you move toward something greater, your field must stretch to hold it. The problem is, most people try to manifest more without ever expanding their receiving structure. They try to fit abundance into a body still bracing for rejection, into a field still coded for scarcity, into a nervous system still wired for survival.

That's why it doesn't stick. That's why the abundance comes, then disappears. It's not a punishment. It's mechanics.

Receiving requires space.

And space must be made—not just in your schedule, not just in your bank account, but in your *energy*. This is the sacred mechanic no one teaches. That receiving is not something you hustle toward or chase down. It's something you *make room for*. You don't attract what you want. You attract what you are willing to *hold*.

And that's where this practice begins.

You must train your body, your field, and your awareness to expand in real time. Not just when it feels safe. Not just when conditions are perfect. But when it feels like too much. When your old programming screams to contract. When your nervous system wants to shut down, apologize, or give it all back.

That's the edge.

The edge is sacred. It's where expansion is either integrated or rejected. And to meet that edge consciously, you need a method—one that works not just on the level of thoughts, but on the level of sensation.

Let's go there now.

Practice: The Energetic Arc of Expansion

This is a tool you can use daily, in real-time moments of opportunity, fear, or resistance. Think of it as a breath-based energetic tuning fork. You are not trying to "force" openness. You are practicing the capacity to *stay* open when your system wants to close.

43

Step 1: Notice the Contraction.

This is subtle but essential. You might feel it as tension in the chest, tightness in the throat, a rush of heat, or an urge to shut down. It can happen in response to praise, to a new opportunity, to the idea of having more. Pause. Don't override it. Don't try to fix it. Just *notice*.

Step 2: Locate the Sensation.

Ask yourself: "Where in my body do I feel this?" It might be a single point or a general heaviness. Get specific. Your body is speaking in sensation. Listening builds trust.

Step 3: Breathe Into the Space.

Place your hand over the area, gently. Inhale slowly, feeling the breath move into that space—not to force it open, but to acknowledge it. Exhale just as slowly, imagining that you're widening the energetic container around it. No rush. No judgment. Just space.

Step 4: Speak a New Signal.

Once your system feels a slight softening, even just 2%, speak aloud (or internally): "I allow myself to receive. I am safe to expand." Choose language that feels alive for you. The words don't matter as much as the energetic tone. You are giving your body *permission* to stretch.

Step 5: Hold the Opening.

Sit in the space you just created. Not thinking. Just being. You may feel tingling, emotion, or nothing at all. That's okay. You are imprinting a new pattern: holding more without collapsing.

If discomfort arises, stay present with it. Discomfort is not a sign to stop. It's a sign that the nervous system is updating its capacity. It means your body is encountering unfamiliar frequencies and trying to map safety in a new space. Most people run from this. They interpret the stretching as a warning rather than a signal of growth.

But you are no longer most people. You are no longer seeking comfort. You are cultivating capacity.

This is how you rewire the energy of receiving from within. No visualization or affirmation will matter if the body cannot hold what the mind tries to call in. Expansion is not something that happens only during rituals or deep practices. It is forged in everyday moments. It's built in how you respond to an unexpected compliment, an invoice paid early, a stranger offering support, an opportunity that feels too big.

Each time, you are offered a choice: collapse or hold.

The field learns through repetition. Each time you hold a little more, stay open a little longer, breathe through the contraction instead of flinching from it, you train your energy to expand as a default setting. You begin to feel less urgency. Less grasping. You stop needing to chase what you are now calibrated to receive.

This calibration becomes magnetic. You no longer need to announce your value. Your field broadcasts it. You no longer need to convince anyone to choose you. The universe responds to your expansion with precision.

And this isn't spiritual poetry. It's energetic precision.

There is a geometry to abundance. A shape to expansion. When your field remains constricted, opportunities pass you by not because they aren't meant for you, but because your system isn't available to receive them. You are full of old signals, old guilt, old tension, old rules. Expansion clears space. It sends a message that your container is clean, available, and ready.

You don't need to force more in. You need to *clear the interference*.

One of the most powerful ways to integrate this is to move the practice from stillness into motion. After you've breathed through the expansion practice, stand up. Let the energy of openness translate into your posture. Let your spine lengthen. Walk through your space slowly, letting the body move from this new signal. This anchors the shift into the physical. It teaches the body that expansion isn't a concept. It's an action.

Small rituals done consistently are more powerful than big rituals done rarely. You don't need an hour. You need three minutes, repeated daily. That's how a new energetic blueprint is installed. That's how you normalize abundance. You don't manifest more by efforting harder. You manifest more by *receiving* better.

When you practice the sacred mechanics of expansion, you begin to notice something strange. The fear doesn't disappear, but it softens. The doubt doesn't vanish, but it loses its authority. You realize that your life was never lacking. It was just compressed. Your field was folded in on itself, waiting for permission to stretch.

And now it's stretching.

You are becoming more spacious than your story. More open than your past. More attuned to the future that has always been reaching for you.

This is the expansion that holds. Not a burst of positivity. Not a temporary high. But a recalibrated state of being. A frequency of enoughness that does not collapse when tested. A field that says yes before the mind has a chance to doubt.

This is not magic.

It's mechanics.

And you are the one who now knows how to work them.

Chapter 3. Wealth Identity Collapse

Dismantling the Identity of the Struggling Seeker

You can't receive what you still believe you're not. And you can't become who you were meant to be if you're still defending the story of who you had to be.

The "struggling seeker" is one of the most seductive and persistent identities in the personal development and spiritual world. It feels humble. It feels noble. It feels like you're doing the work. But in truth, it's an identity built on the energy of lack — not just material lack, but identity-level lack. Always searching, never arriving. Always healing, never whole.

You've probably felt the energetic pull of this identity in the way you speak, the words you choose, the justifications you give for not having what you want yet. It hides in phrases like:

- "I'm still figuring it out."
- "I'm doing the inner work, but it's not showing up yet."
- "I know it's coming, I just have to be patient."

There's nothing wrong with these statements on the surface. But if they become the default narrative, they begin to root you in the role of someone who is always just about to break through — but never quite does. That's not a glitch in your manifestation. That's a reflection of identity.

And identity is the engine of reality.

So before you try to attract more, you must dismantle the structure that unconsciously insists you are still waiting, still fixing, still "almost there."

To begin this process, you must shift your relationship with language. Language is not neutral. It carries frequency. When you repeat stories about how hard it's been, how long you've struggled, how much you've tried, you are reinforcing the neural and energetic pathways of your previous self. You are feeding the identity that believes it must hustle, struggle, purify, or earn. That stops now.

Take a moment and bring to mind a phrase you often repeat when talking about your journey. Something you've said to a coach, to a friend, or silently in your own mind. A phrase that feels "true," but keeps you in limbo. Now ask:

- What identity does this phrase reinforce?
- What role does it keep me locked in?
- Who am I when I say this?

Then go deeper.

- Who would I become if I stopped needing this sentence to be true?
- What part of me might lose its sense of purpose without this struggle?
- What would I do tomorrow if I believed it had already shifted?

This is not about bypassing your story. It's about interrupting your loop.

The struggling seeker survives by narrating its effort. By cataloging every step. By making the healing journey the centerpiece of identity. It is terrified of completion because it doesn't know who it would be without the chase.

That's why dismantling this identity isn't just mental. It has to include the body. You have to *feel* what it's like to no longer belong to the old story. To no longer hold the energetic weight of your own struggle like it's a badge of spiritual merit.

Let's begin this integration now.

Find a quiet space. Sit or stand, but let your spine elongate gently, so your body is open and alert. Bring to mind a moment in your journey where you felt like you were doing everything right, but nothing was shifting. A moment that triggered the narrative of "Why is it not working?"

Without trying to fix or explain it, let the energy of that version of you rise into awareness. Let their posture come back. Let their tone of voice return. Notice how they breathe, how they think, how they move.

Then, speak this out loud:

"That was one version of me. It was real. It was part of the process. But it is not who I am now."

Pause and feel what comes up. Not all of it will be comfortable. That's exactly where we begin.

Let whatever sensations arise move through you fully. Don't rush to shift them. Just observe. This is the residue of the identity shedding. Like dead skin peeling away, it may feel strange or raw, but it is not dangerous. It is the space that opens when you stop defending your suffering.

Now, breathe into your center. Let your body anchor the truth that something has ended. Not because you pushed it away, but because you saw it clearly. And now, we give form to something new.

Speak this:

"I do not need to suffer to be worthy. I do not need to wait to be ready. I am no longer the one who waits to become. I am the one who remembers I already am."

Let that land. Not just as words, but as a frequency shift. Then feel what changes in your body when that becomes your inner tone. This is not affirmation for the sake of positive thinking. It is energetic reorientation.

This is how you begin to walk as a different archetype.

The struggling seeker is constantly calibrating based on lack. Every choice is filtered through "Will this fix me?" The receiving self, the sovereign self, does not seek proof. It moves from inner resonance. It lets desire be enough of a reason.

This shift is not only personal. It's archetypal. You are not just releasing a pattern in yourself. You are interrupting an energetic lineage passed down through generations, especially for those conditioned to associate goodness with struggle, humility with smallness, and transformation with never-ending work.

There's a reason this identity has felt so seductive. It created safety in a world where power often felt punished. As long as you were still struggling, still trying, you were safe from criticism, blame, or the fear of actually having. Because having comes with responsibility. With visibility. With choice.

And choice is a kind of power.

So take this next piece gently, but honestly. Ask:

- *What gets to die when I stop being the seeker?*
- *What fear do I face if I am no longer lost, healing, or almost-there?*
- *What excuses dissolve when I no longer wear effort like a shield?*

Sit with these questions in stillness. Don't answer from your mind. Let your body speak. Often, there's a moment of quiet grief here. That's okay. Identities that kept us safe are still part of our story, even if we no longer carry them forward.

You are not erasing who you were. You are honoring it by no longer needing to live in it.

Now, let's install a new inner structure. Not a fantasy. Not a mask. A grounded, embodied knowing that says:

"I am now the one who walks as if the door is already open."

Let that sentence guide your decisions. Let it shift your posture. Let it alter the way you speak to others, how you invest your energy, and what you allow yourself to receive.

You are not doing the work to become ready. You are doing the work because you are ready.

The struggling seeker looked for permission in the eyes of others. This version of you no longer does. You source from within. You stop asking for time to prove yourself. You stop postponing the moment when your life begins.

And you stop explaining yourself.

That may be the hardest part. When you leave behind the struggle, some people will no longer understand you. They may still be inside that loop. And that's okay. You don't need to rescue them. Your presence will speak louder than your teaching ever could. And when they're ready, they will recognize you not as someone who got lucky, but as someone who chose differently.

This is what it means to collapse the seeker and activate the receiver.

You didn't need to try harder.

You just needed to stop performing the struggle.

Energetic I.D. Theft: How Shame Steals Your Power

Shame is not just a feeling. It is a rewriting mechanism. One that rewires your sense of self, alters your posture in the world, and shrinks your field of receiving without ever asking permission. Unlike guilt, which is about what you did, shame goes deeper. It's about who you believe you are. And the moment shame takes root, your energetic signature starts to change.

It's like someone quietly stealing your identity and replacing it with a forged version. The outer structure may look similar, but the inner code is no longer yours. Your choices become cautious. Your voice grows smaller. Your desires become whispers instead of declarations. And slowly, without even realizing it, you begin to organize your entire life around not being too much, not being exposed, not being seen.

That's the real cost of shame. Not the discomfort. Not the ache in your chest. But the energetic shift that convinces you to shrink your field to feel safe.

This shift happens early, often before we even have language for it. A child expresses joy or creativity and is told they're being inappropriate. A girl speaks up and is labeled attention-seeking. A boy cries and is told to toughen up. These moments may seem small on the surface, but they carry weight. Not because of the words themselves, but because of the energetic imprint they leave. An imprint that says: *who you are is dangerous.*

Shame doesn't need to shout. It operates in silence. In the subtle hesitation before you say what you really think. In the pause before you claim what you want. In the reflex to make yourself smaller when you enter a room. Over time, those micro-adjustments become identity. You forget there was ever another way to be.

That's what makes it so insidious. Shame isn't always loud or dramatic. Sometimes it wears the mask of modesty, humility, or emotional intelligence. But underneath, it's still performing the same role: editing your life so you don't trigger judgment.

Energetically, shame distorts your frequency by pulling your power inward and downward. Instead of letting your energy expand and move outward into creation, it recycles itself into internal doubt. Instead of signaling strength and receptivity, your field broadcasts hesitation. You become a magnet for misalignment. Not because you're broken, but because shame has convinced your system that visibility is a threat.

Real-world example: Think of someone walking into a room who doesn't feel they belong there. They may smile, say all the right things, wear the right clothes. But their field gives off a different signal. One of contraction. One of apology. One of energetic fragility. And that signal shapes how others respond to them. Not because people are cruel, but because energy responds to energy. If your frequency says, "I don't really believe I belong," the world tends to mirror that back.

Shame also hijacks your relationship with desire. When you feel ashamed, wanting becomes dangerous. You second-guess it. You downplay it. You tell yourself to be grateful for what you already have, even when part of you is aching for more. And over time, this creates a split between your inner truth and your external expression. That split weakens your field. It leaks your energy. And it reinforces the lie that what you want is too much, too fast, or too selfish.

The most damaging part of this pattern is how often it disguises itself as maturity or morality. Shame wears the face of being "realistic." It wraps itself in spiritual humility. It teaches you to lower your expectations in the name of growth, when in reality, it's just keeping you compliant.

That's why shame isn't just a personal wound. It's an energetic tactic. A tool of suppression encoded into cultures, families, religions, and social systems that benefit from your smallness. Because a person anchored in unshakable inner truth is hard to manipulate. But a person who quietly questions their worth will mold themselves into whatever shape they think will earn love, safety, or belonging.

The first step in reclaiming your power is to notice the places where shame still speaks for you. The parts of you that lower your gaze, soften your voice, or smile when you want to roar. And not with judgment, but with radical clarity. Because once you see it, you can't unsee it.

The real tragedy of shame is that it convinces you to become the guard of your own prison. You start censoring yourself before anyone else can. You adjust your words, your tone, your timing. You scan every space for permission. Not because you lack intelligence or strength, but because some part of you has internalized the belief that expression equals danger.

And this isn't just mental. It's energetic. Your body becomes fluent in contraction. Your nervous system fires preemptively when you approach your edges. You unconsciously tense up when it's your turn to receive. The opportunity shows up, and your field closes by the time it reaches you. Not because you didn't want it, but because shame convinced you you weren't ready. Or worse, that you didn't deserve it.

The mind will rationalize all of this, of course. It will call it patience. Humility. Maturity. It will dress up the contraction as wisdom. But the body always knows. The energy always tells the truth. And if you tune in, you'll feel it. That subtle pulling inward, the invisible barrier between you and the life that's trying to meet you. That isn't intuition. That's programming.

One of the most potent things you can do is begin to unhook your self-worth from the false morality of shame. Not by fighting it, but by seeing it. By recognizing where its voice has merged with your own. It often sounds reasonable, even loving. That's how it works. Shame rarely arrives in the form of self-hatred. It arrives as self-protection. As carefulness. As responsibility.

But look closer and you'll see the pattern: every time you approach more aliveness, more visibility, more expansion, shame offers a reason to pause. To shrink. To wait. That's not intuition. That's a leash.

Reclaiming your power means breaking the contract. The one you never consciously signed, but have honored for years. The contract that says, "If I stay small, I'll be safe. If I stay humble, I'll be loved. If I stay quiet, I'll be accepted." These aren't facts. These are energetic agreements formed in a state of vulnerability. And the moment you see them for what they are, you can decide whether to keep them.

You don't heal shame by overcompensating with performance or proving. That just adds more weight to the illusion. You heal shame by reestablishing energetic truth. By speaking from the center of yourself, even if your voice shakes. By claiming what you want, even if no one else claps. By no longer outsourcing your belonging to the people who only approve of your edited self.

This is not about becoming loud or aggressive. It's about becoming whole. The kind of whole that no longer fragments itself to fit into places where authenticity is inconvenient. The kind of whole that no longer makes apologies for its fire.

Power begins to return the moment you stop negotiating with shame. Not because it disappears, but because it loses influence. You stop letting it steer. You stop mistaking it for conscience. You stop calling it spiritual.

And once that happens, your field recalibrates. You no longer emit the frequency of self-doubt or subtle apology. You begin to attract people, situations, and opportunities that match your unedited essence. Not the version of you that performs safety, but the version of you that breathes freely, moves boldly, and knows her presence is not a threat to anyone who is truly aligned.

Shame is not just emotional weight. It is energetic distortion. And it doesn't leave with logic. It leaves when your frequency becomes incompatible with it. That happens through clarity. Through choice. Through a quiet refusal to carry what was never yours.

What returns in its absence is not just confidence, but sovereignty. A way of walking that does not wait for permission. A presence that does not apologize for taking up space. A life that no longer orbits the opinions of those who are still afraid of their own power.

You don't have to fix shame. You just have to stop believing it's telling the truth. The moment you do, the energy that once kept you small begins to rebuild your real identity. One that was never meant to be hidden. One that was never meant to feel like too much. One that was waiting, all along, for you to come back to yourself.

Building the Self-Image of a Natural Receiver

There's a version of you that doesn't flinch when goodness enters. She doesn't second-guess when blessings arrive early or stay longer than expected. She doesn't shrink in the presence of praise, or question if she's taken up too much. She doesn't mentally calculate whether she's "earned" the joy or whether it will be taken away to restore some invisible balance. She receives like it's the most natural thing in the world. Because for her, it is.

Most people try to *achieve* that version of themselves by striving. By visualizing more. By trying to attract from a place of hypervigilance and performance. But the energy of trying to *become* a receiver is already a signal that you are not one. And your subconscious doesn't follow words. It follows the feeling underneath them. If the feeling is "I am not yet worthy," then no amount of declarations or affirmations will create a different result. This is where identity enters. Not as a mental image, but as a frequency. And identity does not shift with effort. It shifts with embodiment.

To become a natural receiver, you must begin to relate to yourself differently. Not as someone "doing enough to be chosen," but as someone who is already seated at the center of her field, already tuned to the language of life's offerings, already willing to hold what others deflect. This doesn't require fixing yourself. It requires remembering what you were before the shame, before the guilt, before the programming. That self is not lost. She's simply buried.

To bring her to the surface, you need a ritual that speaks her language. One that doesn't just change how you think, but how you walk, breathe, respond. Because receiving is not a concept. It's a physical posture. A subtle availability. A nervous system that says yes.

The following practice is not a formula. It's a ritual. One you return to daily, not to get somewhere, but to keep remembering. It works not because of what it does, but because of how it orients you back to truth.

The Receiving Mirror Ritual

Begin by choosing a time each day when the world is quiet. Early morning before the world lays its weight on you. Or late at night, when the noise has finally dimmed. Make it a sacred space. Not just a bathroom mirror. Not just a quick glance. Create an altar with your attention.

Stand in front of the mirror and look directly into your eyes. Not your hair, not your skin, not the things you'd like to fix. Look into the part of you that never changed. The one that remembers.

Let the silence stretch longer than what feels comfortable. Don't fill it with words yet. Just presence. Just witnessing. So much of your life has been spent in output — performing, pleasing, producing. This is a space of return. A space of listening.

Now, speak to yourself as the one who receives. Not the one who is *trying* to receive, but the one who already is. Speak as her. In her tone. From her stance. You might say:

I am the one who receives with ease.

I do not brace for loss.

I do not ask permission to keep what arrives.

I trust what wants me.

I trust what stays.

As you speak, watch your body. Notice the places that tense. The parts that want to look away. The urge to rush. These are the remnants of your old identity. They are not obstacles — they are signals. Witness them without judgment. Then soften.

Let your shoulders drop. Let your breath deepen. Let your hands unclench. You are teaching your nervous system that receiving is not a threat. You are anchoring a new default. One breath at a time.

Let your entire body become a yes. A soft yes, not one that grasps or clings, but one that simply remains open. A yes that doesn't need to hustle to prove its worth. A yes that doesn't apologize for existing. This is the frequency of a natural receiver. It is not loud. It does not demand. It does not rush. It holds. It allows. It welcomes.

Now close your eyes. Bring into your awareness one thing you're calling in. Not as a wish, but as a certainty. See it not in the future, but already arriving. Imagine how it feels to receive it with no resistance. Let it sit in your hands, in your chest, in your field. Let yourself hold it without guilt. Without shrinking. Without waiting for the other shoe to drop. Stay in that feeling. Let it stretch wider than your fear of losing it.

You are not just visualizing the thing. You are anchoring the version of you that naturally receives it. The version of you that makes it feel at home. Because anything that feels foreign to your identity cannot stay. The work is not to get more. The work is to become the one who knows what to do with more. Without flinching. Without flailing. Without forgetting who she is when it arrives.

If tears come, let them. They are not weakness. They are release. Layers of old definitions peeling off. Versions of you who lived too long in survival saying their final goodbyes. Make space for them. Then return your awareness to the new one emerging. The one who no longer seeks proof before she allows fullness.

When you open your eyes again, stay with yourself. No rushing away. No collapsing back into the old rhythm. Let your next movement be deliberate. Choose what you wear, how you walk, how you speak, from this energy. Let this identity bleed into everything. How you answer messages. How you say no. How you say yes. How you hold space for others without abandoning yourself.

This is not about pretending to be confident. It's about being congruent. You are no longer playing the role of someone becoming. You are embodying someone who already is. There's no striving in that. Only remembering. Only returning.

You may notice subtle discomfort in the days after you begin this ritual. Not because it isn't working, but because it is. Your nervous system may try to shrink you back into familiar doubt. Your old identity may whisper that this is delusion. That you're making yourself too visible. Too big. Too soft. Too certain.

But the version of you who thrives is not at war with her receiving. She does not equate comfort with complacency. She does not link humility with lack. She knows that her fullness is not a threat to others. It is a mirror of what is possible.

She does not take only what she needs. She receives what is aligned. And that distinction changes everything.

Every time you meet yourself in the mirror, you are building this version. Not with force, but with presence. You are showing your subconscious that receiving is safe. That your nervous system can hold more without collapse.

That your desires are not demands — they are invitations. And you are ready to say yes.

The world reflects not what you beg for, but what you believe you are allowed to have. This ritual rewrites that belief. Slowly. Powerfully. Permanently. Not by convincing your mind, but by speaking to your body in a language it understands.

And in time, you will find that the version of you who receives with ease is no longer something you visit. She is simply who you are. Quietly. Fully. Unapologetically.

This is how receiving becomes a way of being. Not because you finally earned it, but because you finally remembered it was yours all along.

Chapter 4. Nervous System Alchemy

Somatic Resistance to Expansion

You might say you want more. More ease. More wealth. More recognition. But wanting happens in the mind, and receiving happens in the body. The two don't always agree.

This is where most people get stuck. Not because they don't visualize clearly enough, or journal consistently, or want it bad enough. They get stuck because their body flinches at the idea of expansion. Not consciously. Not loudly. But subtly, through tension, hesitation, and retreat.

Your nervous system is not loyal to your desires. It's loyal to your patterns. And if your body has been conditioned to associate more with danger, exposure, loss, or overwhelm, it will quietly sabotage what you say you want in order to keep you safe. Not thriving. Not fulfilled. Just safe.

This isn't dysfunction. It's protection. And it's often so seamless you won't even know it's happening. You'll just feel tired when the opportunity comes. You'll procrastinate on sending the email. You'll forget to follow up. You'll get sick the week of the launch. You'll "just not feel ready." And these moments will feel logical. Reasonable. Rational. But they are echoes of a deeper imprint that says, *if I expand, I will be unsafe.*

The body remembers what the mind tries to forget. That time you were celebrated and then punished. That time you got the thing and then lost it. That time you asked for more and were told you were ungrateful. These imprints don't stay in your conscious thoughts. They stay in your fascia, your breath, your gut.

So when you start to call in expansion, your body doesn't respond to the dream. It responds to the memory.

It says, "Last time we got close to this… something bad happened." It tightens. It slows you down. It contracts. Not because you're broken. Because your body loves you. It just doesn't know yet that expansion can be safe now.

This is why mindset work, on its own, often falls short. You can repeat affirmations all day, but if your jaw is clenched, your belly is tight, and your shoulders are carrying a quiet panic, the body will win. Every time.

Somatic resistance isn't always dramatic. It's not a full-blown panic attack or physical illness. Sometimes it looks like slight nausea when you think about raising your prices. A wave of exhaustion when you consider visibility. A tightening in your chest when you say "yes" to something big. That's the body voting against the future you've said you want.

It's not trying to sabotage you. It's trying to protect a version of you that lived through less. It remembers how to survive, not how to receive.

Expansion requires more than permission from the mind. It requires safety in the body. Until that safety is established, the body will push back. It will shrink what tries to grow. It will resist what tries to enter. And not because you're not meant for it — but because you haven't shown your body that it's not the enemy.

You can't bully the nervous system into submission. You have to partner with it. Speak its language. Teach it slowly that overflow doesn't mean danger. That being seen doesn't mean abandonment. That wealth doesn't mean betrayal. The more you do this, the more your body stops bracing and starts softening.

This is the real energetic work. Not just calling things in, but making your system a place where those things can land and stay. A place that doesn't flinch. Doesn't brace. Doesn't shut down under the weight of more.

Your next level is not waiting for you to be more spiritual or more strategic. It's waiting for your body to stop confusing growth with threat.

You don't need to override the fear. You need to retrain the signal. Every time your body contracts in response to possibility, that's not failure. That's a conversation. It's an invitation to pause, breathe, and let the body know you're not abandoning it to reach your next level. You're taking it with you.

Expansion that bypasses the body is short-lived. You might land the opportunity, sign the client, get the attention, or receive the windfall. But if your body doesn't feel safe holding it, it will find ways to lose it. That's why you see people rising fast and crashing hard. There was no nervous system capacity built. No integration. No true holding. Just reach, grab, collapse.

You're not here to collapse. You're here to expand with sustainability. That means training your system to hold more through micro-moments of regulation. When the email comes in that triggers doubt, breathe. When your voice starts to shake on the live video, stay. When you feel the pull to shut it all down, place a hand on your body and anchor in the now. This is the work. Not resisting the resistance, but becoming skilled at staying with yourself through it.

Every time you stay, your body learns that it's not alone. That it's not being dragged through another unsafe threshold without support. And little by little, it stops bracing. It stops sounding the alarm. It learns how to hold more without collapse.

There's a pace at which your body can integrate your expansion. If you go too slow, you stagnate. If you go too fast, you fry the circuit. The art is to listen for the edge — not the comfort zone, not the panic zone, but the alive edge where growth and safety are both present. That's the place where real transformation happens. Not in the extreme, but in the precision.

You don't need to prove that you can handle more. You need to feel what it's like to hold more and stay open. That might mean saying no to urgency and yes to calibration. Not waiting, but preparing. Not pushing, but strengthening.

When you do that, abundance doesn't shock your system. It settles in. It's not a flood. It's a current. Something that flows through a channel you've prepared. Something that doesn't feel foreign or dangerous or destabilizing — because your body recognizes it. Not as a threat, but as a match.

This is where somatic sovereignty begins. When you are no longer hijacked by old responses. When your body doesn't retreat every time life offers more. When your nervous system becomes a container for expansion, not a cage for contraction.

If your patterns of resistance were built slowly and subtly, your path to expansion can follow the same rhythm. That's not weakness. That's mastery. Meeting the body where it is, without rushing, without shaming, without making it wrong. Only showing it, moment by moment, that the world is not what it was, and you are no longer who you had to be.

Your body doesn't just house your power. It *is* your power. When it opens, life rushes in. But if it closes — no matter how clear your intentions — nothing lands. So your work isn't to try harder. It's to become the kind of vessel that no longer leaks power at the threshold of abundance.

Expansion doesn't require aggression. It requires intimacy. With your patterns. With your nervous system. With your own body's truth. That's how the field is expanded — not through force, but through safety. Not by bypassing, but by honoring. And when that happens, you no longer have to chase more.

You simply become the one it can find.

Safety, Capacity, and Subconscious Shutdown

You don't sabotage your own abundance because you're weak or lazy or unworthy. You do it because your system doesn't feel safe holding more.

Abundance isn't just a mindset. It's a frequency that your entire being needs to hold. And the nervous system is the gatekeeper. If your subconscious registers more visibility, more money, more intimacy, or more power as dangerous, it will shut the door before it ever reaches you. Not because it's against you, but because it's trying to protect you from what it doesn't yet believe is survivable.

This is why affirmations often fall flat. You can repeat "I am worthy of wealth" a thousand times, but if your body is bracing for danger every time you receive, you'll unconsciously block, reject, or spend it away just to get back to your baseline of safety. This isn't failure. It's a brilliant form of survival.

Capacity is the space in your system to hold, process, and integrate more without collapse. It's not built through pressure. It's built through safety. You cannot stretch what you do not feel safe inside. And that's where most people unknowingly disconnect. They try to force themselves into expansion by pushing, hustling, or chasing the next strategy, thinking that more effort equals more results. But the truth is, expansion without regulation equals shutdown.

Regulating your nervous system is the foundation for holding more. And it starts with learning to detect the signs of subtle shutdown: procrastination, sudden fatigue, looping thoughts, breath holding, impulsive spending, checking out, or self-isolation. These aren't random behaviors. They're signs that your system has hit a threshold.

Instead of judging these moments, use them as cues. Your body isn't betraying you. It's alerting you. Something about this moment feels unfamiliar, and the subconscious is trying to return you to what it believes is "safe," even if that "safe" is lack, struggle, or hiding.

This is where the real work begins — not by overriding, but by increasing safety in real time.

Start here:

Create Micro-Containers of Safety

Pick one area where you desire expansion. Maybe it's being seen online, asking for higher rates, or allowing yourself to receive help. Don't jump into the most extreme version of that scenario. Instead, find a micro-version. Something small enough that it activates just a slight edge, but not so much that it triggers shutdown.

For example, if going live terrifies you, start with recording a short voice note on your phone just for yourself. Let your nervous system feel what it's like to express without consequence. Let it associate self-expression with neutrality, or even pleasure. Once that feels safe, move to the next step: a short video to a trusted friend. Then maybe a post. Then maybe a live.

This gradual increase is not playing small. It's building actual capacity. And what you're doing, layer by layer, is pairing new experiences with safety instead of fear. You're reconditioning your body's responses so it stops seeing growth as danger.

Regulate Before, During, and After Receiving

You don't just need to be regulated to *get* what you want. You need to be regulated to *hold* it. That means noticing the moments where abundance tries to enter and your body subtly resists. The compliment that makes you tense. The payment that arrives and instantly triggers guilt. The opportunity that shows up and makes you want to disappear.

Your role is not to shame yourself for those reactions. It's to breathe with them. To anchor presence into the moment. To let your body feel supported enough to hold what's arriving, without needing to eject it for relief.

Notice what the body does in these moments. Not the mind, which may still say "I want this," but the body, which might clench, pull back, dissociate, or go into hyper-control. These are old defense patterns surfacing, not as enemies, but as signals. When you respond with presence instead of panic, the body learns that receiving is no longer unsafe.

One of the most powerful tools for building capacity is conscious pacing. Expansion is not about how fast you can leap. It's about how well you can stay connected while you do. If your nervous system can remain open while you're receiving more than ever before, that's growth. If it collapses under the pressure of performance, it will sabotage itself to return to familiar ground.

This is why many people cycle through success and loss, love and heartbreak, abundance and scarcity. The pattern isn't random. It's a regulation issue. Their identity has outgrown its capacity. The subconscious isn't yet convinced it's safe to stay in that new frequency. And so, even with effort and discipline, they unconsciously return to the previous baseline. The gain disappears, but not because the desire was false. The nervous system simply wasn't on board.

If you've ever felt like you were "almost there" again and again, but something invisible always pulls you back, this is why. Until the body feels safe sustaining the new level, the subconscious will find ways to bring you back to what it knows. Not because you're broken, but because you're wired to survive.

What builds new wiring is consistency of presence, not intensity of effort. The more often you can meet yourself in the edge of discomfort with calm instead of control, the more your system rewires. Breath, sound, touch, grounding, movement. These are not luxuries. They are tools of capacity. They are reminders to the body that sensation is not threat, that growth is not danger, and that expansion can be anchored rather than feared.

A regulated nervous system doesn't mean you're always calm. It means you're aware. It means you can feel intensity without collapsing into it. You can witness contraction and still choose to breathe. You can feel fear and still stay present. That is what creates space for more.

If your nervous system has been conditioned to equate having more with being more responsible, more visible, or more attacked, then it will resist the very thing you're asking for. Not because it hates you, but because it loves you. And love without safety becomes limitation.

So you teach it. Not through force, but through experience. You teach it that joy is safe. That success doesn't mean loss. That money doesn't always come with strings. That being seen doesn't mean being judged. You teach it through moments of pleasure, through presence in the mundane, through rituals of grounding, through the gentle unwinding of false associations that once kept you safe but now keep you small.

Capacity is not a final destination. It's a relationship. You don't earn it once. You build it moment by moment, by choosing not to abandon yourself when your body says, "This feels new and I don't know if we're okay." You pause. You anchor. You stay. And in that staying, something reconfigures.

Not just mentally, but somatically. Your system learns that this level is survivable. And then, over time, it becomes natural.

This is the difference between those who grow sustainably and those who spike then crash. One chases expansion at the cost of presence. The other builds presence until expansion becomes inevitable.

Safety is not a detour from the path. It is the foundation of it. Build it well, and everything you asked for will find somewhere to land. Not in theory, but in your actual life. Not for a moment, but for good.

Daily Calibration Rituals for Energetic Wealth Holding

Wealth is not only built through action. It is held through energy. And energy doesn't calibrate itself once and stay that way. It fluctuates. It responds to the body, the mind, the environment, the emotions, the memories, and the choices made each day. You are always broadcasting something. The question is whether you are broadcasting safety, openness, and readiness to receive, or whether you are unknowingly reinforcing patterns of delay and denial.

To hold wealth energetically is to become someone the nervous system trusts to steward more. This cannot be faked through mindset alone. It must be anchored into daily rhythm, through consistent recalibration. Without daily regulation, expansion often slips into chaos. But with it, your system learns to recognize abundance not as a rare peak, but as a natural resting place.

Ritual is how the energy body remembers. And when ritual is consistent, even simple acts become commands to the field. You don't need to do hours of inner work every day. You need a few precise calibrations that signal to your system: "It is safe to hold more. It is safe to be seen. It is safe to receive."

Below are three core rituals designed to do just that. They are simple, but when done consistently and with full presence, they begin to reshape the subtle code that governs how your reality responds to you.

1. Grounding Through Choice and Stillness

Before your day begins, take a moment before any external input. No phone, no to-do list, no checking. Just sit, stand, or lie still and place a hand on your body. Feel the ground beneath you. Feel where your body meets the earth or the chair or the floor. Breathe slowly. Then speak one sentence aloud: "I choose to hold more than I ever have, with peace in my body."

This phrase is not about repetition for repetition's sake. It is about linking your nervous system to the identity of someone who chooses to hold wealth, not chase it. Stillness at the beginning of the day reinforces safety. Choice activates ownership. Presence in the body neutralizes threat.

If practiced consistently, this becomes a powerful reset each morning. The ritual doesn't take more than two minutes, but those two minutes are the difference between broadcasting reactivity or receptivity for the entire day.

2. Energetic Sweeping to Release Accumulation

Throughout the day, your body picks up signals, projections, and subtle energies that are not yours. These include tension from others, doubts absorbed through media, or old fear that rides in on familiar triggers. By the end of the day, you may feel energetically cluttered without even realizing it. This creates static in your receiving field. And static disrupts signal.

In the evening, use a short energetic sweep to clear this buildup. Stand or sit upright and move your hands from your head downward toward your feet, lightly brushing your energy field. As you do, speak softly: "Anything not mine, I release now. Anything that dims my signal, I let go."

This simple act recalibrates your field. It does not need candles or incense or crystals unless you feel called. The power is in your intention and the embodied movement of release. The body responds quickly to repeated language and motion when they are infused with presence. After the sweep, pause for one minute and ask yourself: "Do I feel safe to receive tomorrow?" If the answer is no, explore why, without judgment. If the answer is yes, let that yes imprint deeply before sleep.

3. Touchpoints of Wealth in the Mundane

So much of your energy is lost trying to make wealth feel far away or exceptional. But wealth isn't an event. It's a field you enter. And to hold it, you must build pathways to it in the ordinary. Small acts done with attention can become magnetic.

Touchpoints of wealth must be placed inside what already exists. When you drink water, notice how generously the earth gives. When you move through your home, notice one object that reflects comfort or beauty. When you speak, speak one phrase as if you already live in the field of wealth. "Everything I touch grows." "My life responds to my energy." "Receiving is natural to me." It doesn't matter which phrase you choose. What matters is that it isn't performative. It must be felt.

Embedding wealth codes into the ordinary rewires the subconscious to expect abundance, not perform worthiness for it. The nervous system needs repeated exposure to familiar safety in order to hold expansion without collapse. These small moments act as scaffolding. They teach your body that wealth does not require proving, stretching, or overreaching. It simply requires capacity, calibration, and continued presence.

Calibration also means listening. If your system begins to contract, you do not force it open through affirmation or push. You attune. You pause. You ask what part of you feels unsafe to grow, and you meet it with regulation. Not correction, not judgment. Presence. Wealth holding begins with nervous system fluency. The more fluently you can read your own signals, the more easily you can return to readiness when it falters.

Some days, your calibration rituals will feel easy. Others, they may feel dull or disconnected. This doesn't mean they aren't working. The ritual is not meant to create fireworks. It is meant to train your energy to stabilize at a higher level of receiving. On the days when it feels mechanical, your consistency is doing invisible repair work beneath the surface. The current is still being redirected. The signal is still broadcasting.

You are not training your mind to think about wealth. You are training your field to hold it without defense. Without shrinking. Without compensation or apology. Daily calibration rituals become the practice of subtle self-leadership. They reinforce your capacity to direct the tone of your energy, to re-enter coherence, and to signal abundance through presence rather than urgency.

You'll start to notice how reality responds differently when these calibrations are in place. Messages arrive with more clarity. Invitations come without forcing. Moments of decision carry more certainty. This is not magic. It's energetic congruence. When your inner field signals openness, steadiness, and coherence, your outer world cannot help but organize itself in response.

Over time, these rituals will evolve. You may feel called to add breathwork, movement, or sacred objects. You may strip everything down to silence and one word spoken into the morning. There's no fixed formula. What matters is that the ritual *lands*. That it connects you back to the truth: you are safe to hold wealth. You are able to increase capacity. You are trusted by your own nervous system to receive and not collapse.

This is what separates those who chase wealth from those who hold it. One builds velocity but lacks containment. The other moves slower but holds more. True abundance expands from a foundation that is repeatedly stabilized, not just momentarily accessed.

Let your life become the altar. Let your breath become the ceremony. Let your quiet, consistent rituals become the signal that reshapes your field. Not because you are trying to get somewhere, but because you are remembering what was always yours to hold. The body knows when it is finally safe. The field knows when you are finally ready. And the moment you treat wealth not as an exception, but as a frequency you calibrate to daily, it arrives without resistance.

You do not need to try harder to be ready. You need to remember that you already are. Then practice holding that remembrance, every single day.

Part II. Activating the New Identity

There comes a moment on the path of reclamation when healing is no longer enough. When clearing, rewiring, and understanding begin to feel complete. When the old self is no longer running the show, but the new self hasn't fully arrived. This is the space between: the liminal edge where an identity has been stripped but not yet rebuilt. Many stay here for years, not realizing that this pause is not destiny. It's an invitation.

Activation begins when you stop defining yourself by what you are no longer, and start embodying who you have decided to become.

Part I was the purge. The dismantling. The removal of unconscious blocks, ancestral patterns, and conditioned contractions that once distorted your capacity to receive. It was about returning to energetic integrity. But clearing the channel is not the same as owning the signal. The second phase is about conscious occupation. It's about embodiment. You are not just healing from a false identity. You are stepping into the frequency of who you were always meant to be: a natural receiver, a grounded holder of wealth, a sovereign architect of your own energetic field.

This part is about precision. Not just feeling ready, but behaving from that readiness. Not just affirming worth, but acting like someone who remembers it at a cellular level. You are not here to endlessly process the old. You are here to install the new. And identity is not installed through words. It's encoded through repetition, ritual, attention, and energy.

You don't shift into a new self by thinking differently. You shift by *being* differently—on a nervous system level, a behavioral level, and an energetic level. The new identity must not only feel true. It must *be lived as truth*.

This is not about pretending. It's about anchoring into a version of you that already exists within your field, waiting for permission to lead. You're not inventing a persona. You're remembering a frequency. And that frequency holds very specific behaviors, boundaries, and expectations. It walks differently. Speaks differently. Decides differently. It doesn't seek proof that abundance is coming. It assumes it already has.

This part will ask for more of your presence, not more of your effort. It will require that you let go of subtle self-sabotage cloaked as humility. It will

71

reveal the habits that contradict your identity and ask you to choose coherence instead. This is where embodiment becomes non-negotiable. Not for performance, but for congruence.

Every exercise, practice, and ritual in this section is designed to anchor this version of you into form. Not as a fantasy, but as a lived energetic fact. You'll be guided to act from wealth instead of toward it. To speak from power instead of for it. To move as if the field is already shaped by your presence—because it is.

The old seeker identity will want to return. It will whisper that you haven't earned this yet, that you still need to fix something first. You'll recognize it now. You'll feel the difference between contraction and truth. And you'll choose again. Because the one who receives with grace is not waiting for permission. She is choosing the role she was always meant to play.

The rituals of this part are not extras. They are energetic declarations. Invitations to the field to mirror your new frequency. And once this frequency is stabilized, the outer world will begin to reflect it, not because you forced it, but because you finally became coherent with it.

You are not stepping into the future. You are stepping into yourself.

Let the activation begin.

Chapter 5. Timeline Distortion and Collapse

Quantum Leaping vs. Timid Progress

There's a kind of hunger that builds after years of waiting, searching, almost-getting-there. When the inner work has been done, the blocks have been faced, and the energy feels close—so close it becomes unbearable to remain still. This is the space where the idea of the *quantum leap* becomes magnetic. A sudden shift. A clean break. A portal into an entirely new reality, not through gradual effort, but by collapsing timelines and stepping into something exponentially different.

But the concept of the quantum leap has been watered down. In the echo chamber of spiritual performance, it's become just another aesthetic ideal. "Leap into your next level," they say, as if it's simply about making a bold decision or chanting a more empowered affirmation. In truth, a quantum leap is not glamorous. It's not just a faster version of success. It's a full-body surrender to a frequency you've never stabilized before. It's the death of everything familiar, without the safety net of step-by-step growth. It feels less like leaping and more like free-falling. And the nervous system will try to stop it.

On the other side, we find the equally misunderstood archetype of slow growth. Often seen as timid, hesitant, or lacking belief, slow progress is painted as the fallback plan for those who "don't trust enough." But in reality, slow growth is a sacred rhythm. It is the nervous system's way of creating capacity. It is the body's request for integration. It is the soul's way of ensuring that what's built will *last*, not just arrive.

The paradox is this: the biggest leaps often begin as quiet, subtle calibrations. And the most radical shifts usually require long periods of invisible preparation. They are not opposites. They are partners. The leap and the build. The collapse and the construction. The void and the form.

A true quantum leap only lands when the deeper identity work has already been done. It's not the start of the journey. It's the moment the field catches up to the self you've already become. And sometimes, when we try to leap too soon, it backfires—not because we aren't worthy, but because the foundation can't hold the weight of the new. The leap doesn't stick. It becomes a high followed by a crash.

This is why timid progress gets a bad name. It looks like hesitation, but often, it's regulation. It looks like delay, but often, it's incubation. You are not always meant to break through with fireworks. Sometimes, you are meant to soften into a frequency so fully that it becomes your baseline. Then, when the shift comes, it's not a leap anymore. It's a natural unfolding. What once felt far away becomes obvious. What once felt forced becomes inevitable.

The pressure to leap can create artificial tension in the body. When you're told to just "go all in" without attunement, you override your own capacity. You bypass the very system that's responsible for anchoring the frequency you want to hold. And this bypass creates instability, not expansion.

What the quantum leap symbolizes is the collapse of internal resistance. But this collapse is not a performance. It's not something you force. It happens when all parts of you become congruent with the truth you've already claimed. That congruence might come gradually or suddenly. But the leap is not in the speed. The leap is in the *coherence*.

Coherence is when your thoughts, emotions, beliefs, and body are speaking the same language. It's when the desire for expansion is not countered by hidden fear, resentment, or identity patterns trying to keep you small. Without coherence, you may leap with your mind, but your body pulls you back. You may say the right affirmations, but the energy underneath them feels brittle, disconnected. You may take big actions, but they carry the residue of desperation, not grounded power.

And when you leap from that place, you don't expand. You fracture.

The truth is that the leap is often not one giant moment, but a series of micro-decisions. Every time you hold a new frequency in the face of an old trigger, you leap. Every time you stay rooted in your power when your bank balance tries to shake you, you leap. Every time you speak a new identity into a familiar room that once mirrored your doubt, you leap. The leap is made of a thousand subtle integrations, many of which feel like nothing at all. That's why so many miss them.

If you're chasing the *feeling* of leaping—drama, risk, adrenaline—you may overlook the actual frequency that allows reality to shift. Sometimes, the biggest transformation arrives in stillness. In repetition. In the quiet power of not reacting the same way you used to. And that's not less potent. That's mastery.

It's easy to romanticize the collapse of the old. The idea of burning bridges, cutting cords, leaving everything behind. But destruction alone doesn't create new realities. If the nervous system isn't resourced to hold the aftermath, you'll unconsciously rebuild what you just tore down. That's why people repeat the same cycles with different names. That's why they find themselves in the same place, only with a new coach, a new relationship, or a new affirmation script.

The body needs to *feel* the safety of the new, not just think it. And sometimes, that safety can only be built through slow recalibration. Through staying, regulating, and rewiring. That's where timid progress becomes sacred.

It's not actually timid. It's intelligent.

In fact, what looks like slow growth from the outside is often extremely brave. It takes more courage to sit in the discomfort of transformation without chasing a dramatic high. It takes more presence to meet your resistance gently than to bulldoze through it in the name of progress. There's no badge for that. No spotlight. But it's where the real quantum shift is seeded.

Quantum doesn't mean fast. It means whole. It means full-spectrum. It means totality.

If you want to become the kind of person who holds more, receives more, embodies more—you must be willing to walk both paths. You must be able to leap when the portal opens, and also to stay when the portal asks you to wait. Because the portal is *not* a doorway someone else opens for you. It's one you create from within, when all parts of you agree it is safe to step through.

Sometimes the leap comes disguised as a pause. Sometimes the breakthrough arrives in the moment you no longer need it to come quickly. And sometimes, what you call delay is actually the universe keeping you from collapsing under a reality your energy wasn't ready to hold.

When you understand this, you stop asking, "When will it happen?"

You start asking, "What part of me still believes I'm not ready?"

And in that question, something opens.

The leap begins.

Collapsing Time Through Identity Imprinting

Time doesn't bend for action alone. It bends for identity.

Most people believe that receiving more simply requires doing more, trying harder, or being more consistent. But what actually compresses timelines— what makes a shift happen in days instead of years—is the frequency of who you *are* while you move. Time responds not to effort, but to embodiment. And embodiment begins with identity.

Think of reality as a mirror. It doesn't reflect your desires, your words, or your vision board affirmations. It reflects the subconscious signature of who you believe yourself to be. If you carry the identity of someone who always has to struggle, reality will delay, obstruct, or collapse any expansion that contradicts that self-concept. It's not punishment. It's coherence. Your external is always trying to match your internal blueprint.

So if you want to collapse time, you must collapse the outdated self who keeps it stretched.

This is where identity imprinting becomes the most potent tool in your field. It is not about pretending to be someone else. It is about consciously selecting a version of you that already exists on a higher frequency timeline and *becoming* it now—not in the future, not when the results arrive, not after some external validation, but now. Fully. From the inside out.

The work is not in getting to the goal, but in closing the gap between who you are *being* and the version of you who already has it. That version is not a fantasy. It's a neural and energetic pattern you can start feeding immediately. And the moment you do, timelines begin to collapse. What was once "far away" starts folding into your present. People, opportunities, shifts in perception, even physical changes begin to accelerate—not because you chased them, but because you matched them.

The mistake most people make is waiting for evidence to allow the shift. They think: "Once I have more money, I'll feel abundant." Or, "Once I get the opportunity, I'll feel worthy." But this is like trying to get warm by asking the fireplace for heat before giving it wood. The fire can't burn until you offer it fuel. Identity is the fuel.

So how do you imprint a new identity?

You begin by choosing it. With clarity. Not as a vague affirmation or a hopeful wish, but as a rooted, grounded decision. You decide who you now are—energetically, emotionally, behaviorally. Not just what you want, but who you must become in order to receive it.

Then you anchor it. Not through external goals, but through repetition of felt experiences. You begin to move, speak, and respond as that version. You walk into familiar situations differently. You speak to yourself in new tones. You make micro-decisions that reflect this new self-image, even when no one else is watching. Especially when no one else is watching.

And perhaps most importantly, you hold this new identity even when the old one screams for attention. That voice will come. It will try to pull you back into safety, into logic, into memory. But if you collapse into it, you collapse the timeline too. The choice must be made again and again, not with force, but with quiet certainty.

Let's now walk through a specific method to help you begin imprinting this new identity with precision. We'll approach this not as a mental exercise, but as a full-body recalibration—because the subconscious doesn't learn through words alone. It learns through experience.

Identity Imprinting Method

Start by creating a quiet, undistracted space. You are not here to visualize a fantasy, but to *install* a new energetic blueprint. This isn't about escape or daydreaming. It's about merging with a version of you that already exists in the quantum field and commanding your nervous system to recognize it as real.

Sit upright. Feel your body. Ground your awareness in your spine and breath. Close your eyes, not to drift, but to deepen inward.

Call forward a version of you who already holds what you are calling in. Not the version who is trying to get there, but the one who *already lives there*. The one who breathes ease, who doesn't second guess, who carries a stable, magnetic energy. Observe them clearly: posture, expression, tone, breath, choices. Don't force traits onto them. Let them *reveal* themselves to you.

Once this version is clear, begin to feel the difference in their internal world. How do they move through rooms? How do they respond to uncertainty, to attention, to opportunity? What do they no longer tolerate or entertain? Not as performance, but as a deep energetic boundary?

Now bring that version into your body. Invite them in like you would wear a well-fitting coat. Slow your breath and allow yourself to *become* this frequency. Not by effort, but by access. You are not reaching for it. You are remembering it. It is not a future self. It is a dormant self. A forgotten self. Let your muscles respond. Let your breath change. Let your face shift. Allow every cell to take instruction from this version. Stay in it long enough that it starts to feel not like imagining, but remembering. Your mind might resist. Your old identity might protest. That's proof the imprint is happening. Stay in the new.

To deepen the imprint, speak. Out loud. Let this version speak through you. Say things you've never said. Use language that reflects certainty, openness, quiet power. Feel your vocal cords recalibrate. This anchors the frequency into the throat center, where so much of your receiving circuitry is blocked. Afterward, don't rush back into your default identity. Move slowly. Let the new code sink in. Drink water. Keep silence. Walk differently. Let the world respond to this version of you, even in small ways. It will. That's the feedback loop that accelerates the collapse of time. The more you hold the new identity *without needing proof*, the faster proof will show up.

You are not performing this identity. You are not affirming it into existence. You are surrendering to it as your new normal. This is the shift. This is how you collapse time.

The old self will tempt you with familiar thoughts. It will offer the comfort of timelines where you can't receive, where things take forever, where you get close but not quite. It will ask you to doubt, to delay, to revert. Smile at it. Don't fight it. Just don't obey it.

Every time you choose the new identity, you compress the space between you and the manifestation. You turn waiting into becoming. You turn struggle into recalibration. You make reality answer to a new source code, one written from within.

This is how timelines bend. Not because the world changes first, but because you did. You held the new self long enough that time couldn't help but catch up.

And when it does, it feels like magic. But it was never magic. It was precision. It was identity. It was you.

Decision as Frequency: Becoming the Embodiment

There's a moment, invisible to most, where your life begins to bend in a new direction. Not when the manifestation arrives, not when the money hits the account, not when others start to notice the change. It begins at the point of decision.

But this kind of decision is not just mental. It's not a preference, a wish, or a vague intention. It's not you thinking, "I hope this works," or "Let's see how this goes." A true energetic decision is a frequency. It is a full-body, full-field shift. And when you make it, you are no longer asking. You are no longer seeking. You *become* the thing you were trying to get.

You can feel it when someone has made this kind of decision. Their voice lands differently. Their body speaks without trying. There is no wavering, no waiting for permission, no explaining themselves to people who aren't ready to understand. They're not rushing to act, but they're already operating from the new timeline, before anything has visibly changed.

Most people don't realize how diluted their decisions are. They make choices laced with fear, layered with backup plans, wrapped in conditions. They move forward while still energetically glancing backward. Then they wonder why the universe doesn't respond. The truth is, the field doesn't respond to words or hopes. It responds to coherence. And coherence only arises when your thoughts, posture, voice, and nervous system are saying the same thing.

This is where embodiment comes in.

To embody a decision, you have to *anchor* it. Not in theory, not in a journal, not in a passive thought. You must install it into your physiology, your language, and your presence. You must become the broadcasting tower for a signal that leaves no space for contradiction.

Start with the body. Posture is the first declaration of truth the world sees before you ever speak. If your spine is collapsed, your shoulders tense, or your breath shallow, you are telling the field that uncertainty still lives in you. So before you even speak your decision, correct your physical alignment. Let the spine rise, the shoulders soften, the chest open, and the breath deepen. Don't over-effort it. Just allow the body to remember how it feels to take up space without apology.

Then bring your attention to the core — the area just below the navel, the seat of your personal power. Breathe into this space. Let the breath anchor here. Not just in a shallow way, but deeply, rhythmically. This is where conviction is born. Not in the mind, but in the lower center of the body, where your sense of direction and stability lives.

Now add language. But not in the form of fluffy affirmations. Use *final* language. Say things out loud like, "This is what I choose. It is already done." Avoid vague statements like "I want" or "I'm trying." Those keep you in the frequency of separation. Speak as someone who knows, not someone who's hoping.

Pause after you say it. Let the words settle into your body. Feel for any inner flinch, any micro-tension, any voice that still wants to negotiate. That's your old identity trying to stay alive. Breathe into it. Don't argue with it. Just out-presence it.

This is the threshold moment — where the old wants to pull you back, and the new requires you to stay. Most people leave too soon. They say the words, strike the pose, breathe the breath, but they don't *hold*. They don't linger long enough for the frequency to root.

Hold. Let it root. Let it start to become the new normal, not the exception. You'll know it's working when the old thoughts don't grip you the same way. When hesitation starts to feel foreign. When the body begins to relax *into* the new, not resist it.

You'll also notice subtle shifts in your environment once the decision begins to hold inside you. Conversations feel different. The same content that once resonated might suddenly feel off. Certain people may pull away or test your new stance, not out of malice, but because your frequency has changed and their old dynamics no longer fit. Don't chase after familiarity. This dissonance is a sign that your field is recalibrating.

The embodiment of a decision must be maintained, not revisited. This is where many collapse the timeline they just initiated. They check too often. They re-decide. They seek signs that it's working. But each time you check, you suggest to the field that the decision isn't real yet. Energy doesn't respond to impatience. It responds to consistency. You are either transmitting the signal or you are scanning for feedback. One builds the field. The other weakens it.

So, embodiment becomes a daily practice, not a one-time moment. And it doesn't require hours of ritual. It requires presence. A few seconds of true embodiment throughout your day can do more than hours of passive visualization. This means waking up and *inhabiting* the version of you who already lives in the result. It means walking into your day with the posture of certainty, speaking with the cadence of someone who no longer bargains with doubt. It means responding to challenges from the version of you who already overcame them.

You are not pretending. Pretending implies you're trying to be something you're not. This is not about acting as if. It's about stepping into the truest version of you that your nervous system is finally ready to accept. The reason this works is not magical thinking. It's physics. When you change the broadcast of your field, the quantum mirror has no choice but to reflect it. But the mirror does not reflect immediately. It reflects consistently. That's why holding the decision is more important than making it loudly once.

Language, posture, and breath are only the surface. Embodiment also requires you to collapse the stories that once reinforced your indecision. The reasons you gave for playing small. The narratives about being underqualified, too late, too early, not ready. These stories live in your energetic field like programs running quietly in the background. They do not vanish through logic. They dissolve through irrelevance. And they become irrelevant the moment your identity no longer aligns with them.

This is why identity work is not about rewriting affirmations. It's about choosing new anchors. Instead of constantly trying to reframe old wounds, build reference points that belong to your future self. Dress differently if you need to. Change your environment, your inputs, your pace. Begin to associate your days with the new signal you are choosing to emit. Identity doesn't change in the mind. It changes through repetition and resonance.

One of the most powerful ways to install a new frequency is through micro-decisions. You don't need to take a massive leap every day. But you must do something that affirms the new decision to your body. Maybe it's choosing the higher standard, pausing before reacting, saying no to what you used to tolerate. Every time you align behavior with identity, you reinforce the signal. Every time you bend to your past, you scatter it.

There is nothing fragile about the embodiment of a real decision. It may start subtle, but it's not weak. It's not in need of validation. It doesn't panic when results don't appear instantly. Because it knows. It lives from the knowing, not the waiting. This is the key to becoming the embodiment. Not acting toward the reality, but transmitting from it.

And as you hold this new field, the outer reality begins to bend. Slowly at first, then more visibly. You start to meet the people, see the opportunities, notice the pathways that were always there but were previously invisible to the version of you that hadn't decided yet. This is the difference between trying to create a result, and becoming the frequency that pulls it in without effort.

You do not need to force outcomes. You only need to stay loyal to the identity that lives in the result. The decision is not what starts the change. The decision *is* the change. When you hold it, it holds you.

Chapter 6. The Shame Loop and the Receiving Block

Why Worthiness Work Keeps You Stuck

The idea that you must *feel worthy* before receiving what you desire has become one of the most seductive traps in the self-development world. It sounds noble. It feels intuitive. But beneath its surface lies a subtle sabotage pattern that keeps you looping, always almost ready, never quite arriving.

The truth is simple: you were never unworthy to begin with. Worthiness is not a state to be earned or recovered. It is not a badge given after enough healing, effort, or approval. It is not something that was stolen from you and must now be reclaimed. Worthiness is a concept invented by the mind to explain resistance, and in trying to "fix" it, you accidentally make the illusion stronger.

What most people call "worthiness work" is actually a form of spiritual bureaucracy. It gives you an endless checklist of internal conditions to meet before life is allowed to give you what you asked for. Do you fully love yourself yet? Have you cleared every ancestral wound? Are you free from all insecurity, doubt, or fear?

This system turns healing into a prerequisite for receiving, which means every time you get close to expansion, your subconscious checks the list, finds an imperfection, and delays the manifestation. You begin to equate growth with delay. Abundance becomes a future version of you, forever one breakthrough away.

There is a difference between healing and clearing. Healing says something was broken and must be fixed. Clearing says an old program is still running and must be deactivated. Healing can be a sacred path, but it becomes dangerous when it becomes your identity. If you start to believe that you are a "wounded being becoming whole," you lock yourself into an identity that can never be ready enough. The process becomes the personality.

That's why worthiness work often creates more spiritual tension than relief. It reinforces the belief that your current self is not trustworthy with power, love, money, visibility. That something must change *before* you can step into your next level. But here's the paradox: the feeling of unworthiness doesn't disappear when you heal enough. It disappears when you stop negotiating with it.

Think of a locked door with a sign that says, "You must feel worthy to pass." Most seekers stop here. They turn inward, analyze their wounds, and try to find the missing key. But there is no lock. There never was. The sign is the trap. The more you believe in it, the more you reinforce a false limitation.

You don't have to *be* worthy. You only have to *decide* that worthiness is no longer part of the conversation. You don't need to feel deserving in order to receive. You need to act from the place that knows receiving is a function of resonance, not permission.

When you live from this truth, you stop waiting for your emotions to give you approval. You stop measuring your readiness based on how healed you feel. You no longer view resistance as a sign to delay, but as a natural part of expanding beyond your old framework.

This does not mean bypassing your emotions. It means not allowing them to govern your access to abundance. It means not using "worthiness" as a proxy for your capacity. You might still feel fear. You might still doubt. But you no longer wait for those feelings to vanish before choosing the identity that can hold what you desire.

It's not your wounds that keep you small. It's your loyalty to the idea that wounds define your eligibility for more. Healing is sacred. But it is not required before you walk through the door. The door opens when you realize you're already on the other side.

You do not have to pass a final emotional exam before life lets you receive. The illusion of unworthiness is not a barrier you must dismantle with enough inner work. It's a phantom you stop feeding by refusing to make it real. The moment you stop trying to earn your way in, you're already inside. There is a powerful shift that happens when you stop asking, *"Am I ready?"* and start declaring, *"I'm available."* Availability bypasses the mental gymnastics of healing narratives. It moves you out of psychological delay and into energetic alignment. When you say, *"I'm available,"* you are no longer referencing your past, your self-image, or your internal flaws. You are referencing the now, and now is the only access point to the field of manifestation.

84

This is why so many brilliant, talented, deeply heart-centered people stay stuck. They have internalized the belief that more clarity, more shadow work, more integration is always required before taking the next step. But at a certain point, the next step is not healing. It's choosing. Not the *feeling* of being chosen, but the energetic frequency of choosing yourself before the world reflects it back.

The nervous system learns through repetition and experience, not theory. The more you delay receiving until you *feel ready*, the more you train your body to associate abundance with postponement. You can heal endlessly and still feel like you're never quite there. But when you start acting from the identity that already holds the thing, the body adapts. Fast.

There is a kind of quiet defiance in no longer explaining your readiness. You become unavailable for the mental loop that says, *"Until I feel enough, I'll keep doing the work."* Instead, you decide that the version of you who holds wealth, love, recognition, fulfillment, is not someone you need to become. It's someone you need to stop postponing.

Let it be immediate. Let it be irrational. Let it be without emotional permission slips. Let it feel like you're stepping into shoes slightly too big and trusting that your energy will grow into them. Let it feel edgy, because it should. That edge is the collapse of delay.

Worthiness was never the real measurement. The system wasn't built around deserving. It was built around coherence. The more you embody the signal of already-having, the less the universe needs to "test" you. What most people experience as resistance is simply lag between identity and behavior. The moment you behave like the version of you who already holds it, reality starts to reconfigure.

This doesn't mean ignoring emotional pain or pretending nothing ever hurt you. It means you stop using the hurt as a reason to stay energetically small. You stop performing worthiness like a currency. You stop waiting for the mirror to validate what only you can claim.

The most radical shift you can make is to withdraw from the performance entirely. Stop trying to look like someone who is ready. Stop trying to prove that you've done the work. Stop referencing your emotional landscape as the map for your next move.

Your life responds to who you *are being* in this moment. Not to your story, not to your past, not to your spiritual resume. Just this moment. Right now.

So, if you no longer had to prove your worthiness...
If you no longer needed to clear another thing...
If you no longer waited for the permission of a healed nervous system...
Who would you become today?
Step into that version. Not because you earned it. But because you remembered it was never denied.

Breaking the Cycle of Overgiving and Underearning

There is a subtle trap many people fall into on the path to receiving more. They give too much. Not from generosity, but from unconscious programming. From a belief that more output will eventually earn them permission to receive. The result? They overextend, overdeliver, overperform—while simultaneously underearning, underreceiving, and undervaluing themselves.

The cycle looks noble on the surface. You become the helper, the reliable one, the fixer. You do more than you're paid for. You pour energy into people who haven't asked for it. You say yes when your body is screaming no. All in the name of being good, useful, or spiritual. But behind that goodness is often a hidden transaction: *"If I give enough, they'll see me. If I help enough, I'll be chosen. If I'm generous enough, I'll finally be safe."*

This creates a chronic mismatch between input and output. You give more than is energetically clean, and life mirrors that imbalance by giving you less than you desire. It's not punishment. It's feedback. The universe responds to the energetic template you hold. If that template says, *"My value comes from over-efforting,"* it will reinforce that story. Overgiving becomes a performance of worth, and underearning becomes its echo.

To break the cycle, you don't need to become selfish. You need to become precise. You need to reclaim your right to let your giving be clear, powerful, and clean—without being entangled in hidden hope or unconscious self-sacrifice.

This is not about doing less. It's about doing from a different place. From alignment, not obligation. From overflow, not depletion. From clarity, not approval-seeking. That shift begins by becoming radically honest about your current patterns. And for that, we start with tracking.

Track the Imbalance

Set aside one full day—or even better, a full week—to track where your energy goes. Every interaction. Every "yes." Every task you do that drains you. Every time you say yes when you mean no. Every time you offer support before being asked. Every moment you sense that your giving is disproportionate to the energetic return.

Don't judge it. Just observe. Write it down, or voice record it as you go. You might be surprised by what you find. Patterns that seemed invisible become crystal clear when you put them in front of you.

Ask yourself:

- Did I just offer more than was asked for?
- Did I agree to something I didn't really want to do?
- Did I feel guilty or afraid to say no?
- Did I give hoping to be liked, chosen, or acknowledged?

You're not looking for perfection. You're looking for the root of the behavior. Most of the time, overgiving is not about love. It's about fear. Fear of being seen as selfish. Fear of not being needed. Fear of being rejected if you stop proving your value.

Now that you've tracked the pattern, the next step is to interrupt it.

Interrupt the Pattern

This is where the nervous system comes in. Overgiving is often somatic. It's a reflex, not a conscious choice. You might say yes before your mind has caught up. You might feel a contraction in your chest or a tightening in your gut the moment you try to say no. That sensation is the body holding an old survival strategy. Interrupting the pattern means becoming present to it.

Pause before you say yes. Breathe. Scan your body. Ask yourself, *"Is this coming from love, or is this coming from fear?"* If there's even a sliver of resentment or collapse in your response, stop. Delay the yes. Reclaim the pause.

Breaking the Cycle of Overgiving and Underearning

The pause is where power returns. In that space between stimulus and response, you reclaim your choice. The automatic yes becomes a conscious decision. The learned pattern of giving without checking becomes an embodied moment of truth. It may feel uncomfortable at first. Your body might interpret it as risk. But that discomfort is not danger. It's your nervous system detoxing from a false sense of safety built on being needed.

This is where the rewiring begins.

Every time you choose presence over reflex, you shift the energy. Every time you say no from integrity, even when it trembles, you're teaching your system a new reality: I am safe when I honor my boundary. I am valuable even when I give less. I am allowed to receive without proving.

Now we reverse the loop.

Reverse the Equation

To move out of the overgiving-underearning cycle, you must begin receiving in places where you previously withheld it. And this isn't just about money. It's about recognition, support, time, space, nourishment. It's about letting energy return to you in equal measure. And sometimes greater.

Pick one small area of your life where you chronically underreceive. It might be asking for help when you're used to doing everything yourself. It might be raising your rates, even slightly, instead of over-delivering for free. It might be telling a friend you're not available to talk, instead of holding space you don't have.

Choose one place. Then make a micro-decision that rebalances the scale.

If you do this consistently, your field recalibrates. The people around you adjust. Some may resist the new version of you. That's part of the clearing. Others will rise to meet you, because you've stopped teaching them that your time and energy are cheap.

This is where overgiving becomes obsolete. Not because you shut down your generosity, but because you've elevated the frequency it operates from. It's no longer a survival mechanism. It becomes a clear, clean expression of overflow. And that overflow becomes magnetic.

It's not your job to pour yourself out in order to be chosen. It's your job to choose yourself so completely that you no longer trade energy for validation. Overgiving is a form of chasing. True receivers do not chase. They calibrate.

The Embodiment Shift

To lock in this shift, integrate it somatically. Stand tall. Shoulders back. Hands open, not clenched. Speak your no with clarity. Speak your yes with discernment. Practice saying, out loud, "I do not need to earn what I am already worthy of." Let your body feel what that truth holds.

Then say, "My value is not in what I do. It's in what I hold."

This reprograms the loop. Because a person who truly believes that does not overgive. They don't rush to fill space with performance. They don't mistake depletion for devotion. They choose impact over exhaustion.

Precision over sacrifice. They allow receiving to be the natural result of energetic alignment, not the prize they must hustle for.

You were never meant to earn your way into worth. You were meant to remember it. And from that remembrance, give only what is yours to give. Nothing more. Nothing less. The cycle breaks not when you take less action, but when every action you take comes from wholeness, not hope.

You will feel the difference. So will everyone around you. But most importantly, so will the field of life that mirrors your internal stance.

The moment you stop feeding the pattern, it dissolves.

And in its place, a new rhythm is born—one where you give cleanly, receive openly, and rest deeply in the knowing that your energy is sacred. Your time is valuable. And your worth was never on trial.

How to Deprogram Guilt Around Having More

Guilt is not just a feeling. It is an embedded frequency that silently runs interference every time you try to expand. You might have the strategy. You might have the talent. But if guilt is sitting at the root of your nervous system, the moment more starts to arrive, something inside you quietly pulls the plug.

It's not logical. It's energetic. And most of it was installed long before you had the awareness to say no.

Maybe you grew up watching your parents struggle, and somewhere inside, you swore never to surpass them. Maybe you saw what happened to people who had more—how they were judged, envied, attacked—and you decided it was safer to stay small. Maybe you still carry the stories of your ancestors, who were punished, betrayed, or isolated the moment they stepped into abundance.

Whatever the origin, guilt around having more creates a subconscious ceiling. And as long as it's there, you will keep cycling through patterns that help you survive, but never fully thrive.

To release guilt, you don't need to analyze it forever. You need to interrupt it. You need to expose it in real time. And then you need to replace it with a new energetic protocol—one that allows your body, mind, and field to experience having more as safe, natural, and deeply deserved.

Step 1: Name the Guilt Pattern

The first step is to catch guilt in the moment. Not in theory. Not in memory. But right now, as it surfaces in your daily life.

Guilt often shows up as:

- Downplaying your wins so others don't feel uncomfortable
- Feeling bad for charging more, even when you've outgrown your old prices
- Apologizing for taking up space, time, or attention
- Dimming your joy in front of people who are struggling
- Giving something away just because you feel you "already have enough"

Notice how subtle it can be. You might think you're just being generous, humble, or considerate. But if the core frequency underneath your action is guilt, then what you're actually doing is self-sabotage disguised as virtue.

Start tracking this with brutal honesty. For one full day, keep a private log of every moment you feel yourself shrinking, giving away energy, or holding back your fullness because you "don't want to seem like too much." This is not to shame yourself. It's to bring the pattern into the light.

The moment you name guilt as a program, it starts to lose its grip.

Step 2: Energetic Interruption

Now that you've identified where guilt lives in your behavior, the next step is to break its default loop. This isn't about talking yourself out of guilt with logic. It's about speaking directly to the deeper system that holds it.

When you feel guilt rising, don't justify it. Interrupt it.

Close your eyes. Drop into your body. Place one hand on your chest, one on your lower belly. Breathe slowly, deeply, as if you are reprogramming your inner rhythm. Say these words out loud or silently:

"This guilt does not belong to me. I release the agreement that says I must suffer to belong. I release the belief that says having more makes me unsafe, bad, or alone. I revoke the identity that equates love with limitation. I choose a new reality now."

Let yourself feel the weight of those words as they move through your system. You might feel heat. You might feel resistance. You might feel emotion rise. Don't suppress it. Let the energy move. You are not performing a ritual. You are opening a portal.

Let the breath settle without forcing anything. After you've interrupted the guilt loop, your system enters a space where new wiring can take place. This is where permission begins—not in your mind, but in your field. The nervous system learns by repetition, but it also learns by resonance. So now, we imprint a new resonance: the energetic code of deservedness without justification.

Feel your body supported. Notice the ground beneath you, the air around you, the steady rhythm of your breath. Speak again, this time as if you're not asking for permission, but claiming what has always been yours.

"I am allowed to expand. I am allowed to have more. I am allowed to feel joy, wealth, freedom, and success without guilt. I do not owe anyone my shrinking. I honor others best when I allow myself to rise."

Hold this frequency for at least one minute in silence. Let the words land. Let them echo in the parts of you that have never heard them before. This is not positive thinking. This is frequency recalibration. You are updating the energetic signature that your subconscious broadcasts to the world.

If you do this daily—especially when guilt begins to sneak back in—you begin to establish a new baseline. You stop negotiating with the old pattern. You stop trying to be good through sacrifice. You start becoming whole through truth.

One of the most powerful ways to anchor this is by aligning your external choices with your internal shift. That means saying no when guilt tries to make you overextend. That means raising your prices when you know you've been undercharging. That means letting yourself be seen and celebrated, even when others might project their discomfort.

Each of these is a micro-decision, but they're also acts of self-loyalty. And when you practice self-loyalty consistently, your field becomes magnetic— not because you're trying to attract, but because you are no longer repelling. Remember, guilt often comes from a place of early emotional imprinting. At some point, having needs, desires, or visibility may have felt unsafe. Guilt became a protective layer, convincing you that it was better to stay small than to risk judgment, envy, or rejection.

But now, that protection is suffocation. What once kept you safe is now keeping you broke, tired, or disconnected. And while that realization can sting, it is also the key to liberation.

You are not obligated to carry guilt that was never yours to begin with. You are not required to make yourself uncomfortable just because someone else refuses to rise. You are not here to be relatable through struggle. You are here to become undeniable through embodiment.

Let this be the line in the sand: from this point forward, your expansion is no longer a negotiation. You will no longer explain away your success. You will no longer trade your overflow for approval.

If that means someone doesn't understand you anymore, let them fall away. If it means you walk alone for a season, walk with power. The field always reorganizes around clarity. The people who truly resonate with your new frequency will find you. The opportunities will reshape. The income will recalibrate. But it all begins with the moment you say yes to thriving without guilt.

You do not need to justify having more.

You only need to remember that your abundance was never a crime. It was your original design.

Chapter 7. Rituals of the Buried Feminine

How Stillness Generates Overflow

Stillness is not the absence of power. It is its source. In a world trained to validate noise, motion, and performance, stillness is often misunderstood as laziness or avoidance. But the deeper truth is this: stillness is the frequency where energy gathers, recalibrates, and returns multiplied. It is the field in which overflow is conceived.

When you enter true stillness—not distraction, not numbness, but the rooted presence of being—you stop leaking energy. You stop chasing outcomes. You stop running a thousand micro-calculations in the background, trying to manage other people's perceptions, anticipate rejection, or outwork your own unworthiness. And in that stopping, something ancient reawakens in you.

The feminine current, the receiving current, flows not through force but through gravity. It pulls. It calls. It draws in, not by demanding, but by being undeniably felt. Stillness is the vessel through which this gravity is cultivated. You become magnetic not by trying to pull anything in, but by resting so deeply in your field that the right things begin to orbit you naturally.

And you can feel this in the body. Sit, right now. Let your spine lengthen. Feel the weight of your hips grounding you into the seat beneath you. Drop the tongue from the roof of your mouth. Relax the muscles behind your eyes. Let the tension in your belly soften just a few degrees. Let your arms hang heavier. Let your breath deepen—not because you're trying to control it, but because you're letting yourself be breathed.

This is not about "manifesting" through stillness as a passive strategy. It's about activating a different energetic architecture. You are no longer operating from the survival system that equates value with productivity. You are activating the channel that says: "I am the source. I don't need to hunt for overflow. I *am* overflow."

From this space, decisions become clearer. Ideas arise with a clarity that frantic effort can never produce. The right words, the aligned actions, the next step all come—not from mental strategy, but from the intelligence of your field.

This is what most people miss. They think overflow comes from piling more action on top of action. But that kind of movement is often rooted in fear. Fear of missing out, fear of being behind, fear of being forgotten. Overflow doesn't emerge from fear. It emerges from frequency.

Stillness is what lets that frequency rise. Because in stillness, you're no longer trying to *prove* you're worthy. You're simply *being* what is already whole. And wholeness doesn't beg. It doesn't chase. It doesn't over-explain. It transmits. If you've been taught that only hard work yields results, this can feel like a betrayal of everything you've known. But look closely. What has all that effort really produced? Has it given you more energy or less? Has it brought sustainable abundance or just brief survival wins?

You may start to realize that the very system you were taught to trust is the one that keeps you depleted. And the deeper betrayal would be continuing to run it.

Now, feel into your chest. Notice the space there. Is it tight? Is it guarded? Can you allow it to open just a little more, like a window that hasn't been touched in years? Not to *do* anything. Just to allow your own field to become more spacious.

Stillness is not about waiting for life to happen to you. It's about becoming the space through which life flows *to* you. And that space is cultivated not through logic, but through deep, embodied permission.

Let your breath fall deeper into your belly. No tension, no forcing. Just the gentle return to a natural rhythm. This is the rhythm your body remembers, even if your mind forgot. The rhythm that wealth responds to. Not the rapid staccato of urgency, but the slow pulse of embodied safety.

Stillness, when practiced regularly, becomes a field of calibration. Not just emotionally, but biologically. Your nervous system begins to register that there is no lion at the door, no immediate danger to defend against, no one you must impress in order to deserve rest. And in that realization, your entire internal chemistry shifts. Cortisol lowers. Digestion returns. Blood flows back to your creative centers. The body opens to receive, because it finally believes it is safe enough to.

You begin to notice how much noise you've carried around without realizing it. The obsessive planning, the silent rehearsals of imaginary conversations, the reflexive flinching into problem-solving when something feels uncertain. These patterns are not flaws. They were once protections.

But when left unchecked, they form an energetic wall that keeps the very abundance you're calling in from landing.

Stillness doesn't demand that you fix all of that. It doesn't ask for your effort. It asks for your presence. It lets you witness these patterns without judgment and without needing to intervene. And in that witnessing, the patterns start to dissolve on their own.

You become more sensitive to truth. Not because you're thinking harder, but because stillness sharpens your internal listening. You start to feel the difference between a yes that is coming from alignment and a yes that is rooted in guilt. You begin to say no without explanation. You stop overextending. You trust the pause.

This is where magnetism builds—not from charisma or intensity, but from the clean frequency of someone who is not at war with themselves. The world can feel it. People feel it. You become the one they seek, not because you're louder, but because your field is clearer. You hold something most people are missing: spaciousness.

Spaciousness is not emptiness. It's a signal. It tells the universe that you are ready. Ready to hold more, not because you've hustled for it, but because you've built the internal space to *contain* it. And unlike fleeting wins, that kind of receiving lasts. It doesn't burn you out. It integrates into who you are.

You'll notice you no longer chase ideas. The ideas come. You don't plead for visibility. Your presence speaks for itself. You don't try to fix people to feel needed. You become a mirror that reflects their own power back to them. And in doing so, you conserve your own.

Stillness doesn't mean stagnation. It means the movement is now internal, subtle, intelligent. The river under the surface. The kind of movement that changes the shape of the land without needing to announce itself.

There is no metric for this in traditional systems. No productivity score. No applause. But there is peace. A kind of quiet knowing that what you hold within is already enough. That your energy is your currency. That your field is the invitation.

Practice this stillness daily, even for a few minutes. Not to earn a result, but to remember the frequency that overflow lives in. Let your spine align with gravity. Let your body speak before your mind interrupts. Let your breath move like an ancient language you once knew fluently.

97

Because it is in the quiet, unshaken center of yourself that the world finally begins to respond to you.
Not because you demanded it.
But because you *became* it.

The Power of Lunar Cycles and Inner Seasons

There is an ancient intelligence pulsing just beneath the surface of your life. You feel it in your body's tides, in your emotional ebbs and flows, in the days when your clarity sharpens without trying and the days when you long to pull inward and rest. This is not weakness. It is rhythm. And when you learn to honor this rhythm instead of resisting it, something opens: power, clarity, alignment, flow.

Most people move through their days like machines, detached from the organic wisdom that's constantly whispering through their cells. But true energetic receptivity does not come from constant effort. It comes from knowing when to move and when to be still. When to call energy in and when to release. This is the work of syncing with the lunar cycle and the internal seasons of your body.

Whether you menstruate or not, whether you identify as feminine or not, you carry these cycles within you. The moon pulls on the waters of the earth, and it pulls on the waters within you. Your hormones, your mood, your cravings, your energy, even your voice tone follow subtle patterns that echo this larger dance.

Ignoring these cycles doesn't make them go away. It just makes you miss the opportunity to harness them. When you begin to align your rituals, decisions, and energetic focus with these internal and external tides, you shift from pushing against life to co-creating with it.

You don't have to become a lunar priestess or memorize the names of each moon phase. What matters is cultivating an embodied awareness of the four core stages, both in the moon's rhythm and your body's energetic seasons: new moon (winter), waxing moon (spring), full moon (summer), and waning moon (autumn). Each phase carries its own frequency, gifts, and energetic instructions.

During the new moon or your inner winter, your body wants rest, silence, reflection. This is not the time to launch or expand. It is the time to dream, to vision, to let yourself be empty so something new can gestate. Pushing yourself to perform in this phase can leave you exhausted and energetically disconnected. But if you allow yourself to root here, to take space and listen, the clarity that arises will guide everything that follows.

As the moon waxes or your inner spring arrives, your energy begins to lift. Your mind clears. Your desire to engage returns. This is the phase for initiating, for planting seeds, for acting on the clarity that emerged during your winter. You'll notice that things begin to move with less resistance here. This is a powerful window to set intentions, take strategic action, or begin a new energetic practice.

The full moon corresponds to summer, the peak of your cycle. Expression, visibility, creativity, connection. Your magnetism is high. Your field is more open. This is the time to speak your truth, to share your work, to make bold asks or decisions. But it is also when suppressed emotions can surface powerfully. Instead of judging them, listen. The full moon illuminates what's been hidden. Use that light to release what no longer serves.

The waning moon or inner autumn asks you to turn inward again. This is the season of discernment. Of pruning. Of evaluating what needs to be let go before the next cycle begins. It is not a punishment. It is the refinement that makes space for aligned growth. When you honor this phase, you stop clinging to what has expired. You let things complete. And in that letting go, you prepare yourself to receive again.

You are not meant to be in constant harvest. Expansion without contraction is not growth; it's inflation. When you allow the ebb to have as much value as the flow, your entire nervous system relaxes. Your intuition sharpens. Your body no longer feels like it has to fight to be heard.

Most blocks in receiving come not from a lack of desire, but from trying to receive in the wrong energetic season. Trying to manifest during an inner winter leads to burnout. Trying to take bold leaps during an emotional autumn often results in sabotage or collapse. The energy isn't wrong, it's simply misaligned with the phase. When you understand the map, your timing becomes precise. You know when to rest and when to move. When to dream and when to build. And each phase feeds the next, in a loop of natural overflow.

There is also an emotional intelligence to these seasons. Your inner winter will often surface grief or old wounds you haven't fully felt. Not to punish you, but to clear the field. Your inner spring might bring excitement and self-doubt in the same breath. Your summer could bring unexpected visibility triggers or resistance to being fully seen. Autumn may stir frustration or impatience, asking you to slow down just when you thought you should be speeding up. All of this is part of the recalibration. When you stop labeling these sensations as problems and start reading them as data, your relationship with your inner world becomes one of reverence, not resistance.

Energetic wealth holding requires this level of attunement. You can recite affirmations, journal your desires, visualize millions flowing in, but if you're ignoring the fact that your body is in a rest phase while trying to force action, your field will stay in conflict. The signal becomes scrambled. Your energy says yes, but your body says not yet. The result is stagnation or sabotage, and you might blame your mindset when really it was just a misread of your inner timing.

To integrate this rhythm into your life, begin by noticing. Track your mood, your energy, your cravings, your sleep, your focus. Even a few lines a day. Over time, patterns will emerge. You'll begin to see that your resistance isn't random. Your bursts of creativity are not luck. Your need to withdraw is not weakness. They're markers. Clues. Invitations into deeper alignment.

As you build this relationship, you can begin syncing small rituals to each phase. They don't have to be elaborate. A few minutes of reflection on the new moon. A walk in the sun during your inner spring. A bold conversation or investment during summer. A release letter or bath in autumn. These moments act as energetic calibration points. They remind your system that it's safe to follow the wave. That it's powerful to pause. That true receptivity doesn't mean being open all the time, it means being available in the right time.

This way of living softens the harsh edges of self-pressure. It unhooks you from the toxic productivity loop that tells you you're behind unless you're always achieving. It teaches you to trust your body again. And when your body trusts you, it begins to open. To hold. To receive. Not in a scattered, frantic way, but with grounded capacity.

You were never meant to force abundance. You were meant to dance with it. To move in rhythm with the unseen forces that shape all things. The tides. The moon. The breath. The beat of the soil under your feet. When your life becomes a ritual of alignment with these cycles, receiving becomes inevitable. Not as a chase, but as a return. A remembering of how it was always meant to be.

Daily Receiving Practices to Reopen the Channel

Most people try to manifest wealth by focusing on the asking. They write the goals, speak the affirmations, visualize the outcomes. But the real work of receiving doesn't happen in the request. It happens in the space afterward. The space where you either tense up and block the flow, or relax and open the channel. Receiving isn't a concept. It's a state your body has to know. And if that state has been unfamiliar or unsafe in your past, then you must reintroduce it daily until it becomes second nature again.

Reopening your channel to receiving begins with simplicity. Not elaborate rituals or hours of inner work, but small, consistent moments that signal to your system: "It's safe to open. It's safe to allow." These rituals work not by forcing energy through, but by softening the places that were once braced against it.

The first layer of daily practice is *somatic openness*. This doesn't mean achieving a perfect posture or performing the right move. It means spending a few intentional minutes letting your body register what "open to receive" actually feels like. Try standing or sitting with your palms up. Let your shoulders soften. Breathe in slowly, and as you exhale, feel the weight of your body supported by the surface beneath you. Say quietly, either aloud or in your mind, "I am safe to receive." You're not trying to convince yourself. You're letting the words land in your cells, like a tuning fork reminding your system of a frequency it once knew.

Even thirty seconds of this practice, done consistently, begins to shift your field. It creates a new baseline of safety. Not only because of what you're doing, but because you're showing up for it every day. Repetition is not just about discipline. It's how the nervous system learns to trust that a new pattern is not a threat.

The next layer is *symbolic receptivity*. This engages the subconscious through action. You can think of this as energetic mimicry. When you engage in a physical ritual that mimics the act of receiving, the body starts to wire that pattern more deeply. One of the simplest forms of this is receiving something intentionally, even if it's small and ordinary. Let someone hold the door open for you without apologizing or deflecting. Accept a compliment without explaining it away. Take a deep breath and let it fill your lungs without restriction, then say, "I allow it to be this easy." Each of these is a form of ritual, even if it doesn't look like one. They are cues to your system that the act of receiving can be casual, effortless, and safe.

You can also introduce a physical object into your ritual space that represents receiving. A bowl, for example, placed somewhere visible, with the intention that it symbolizes your open hands. At the end of each day, you can place something into it—a coin, a flower, a small note of something you allowed in. This is not about superstition or magical thinking. It's about teaching your body that you are no longer closed. That you are tracking what comes in. That you are available, awake, and holding the frequency of someone who allows.

Let your awareness land on what you *didn't* block today, no matter how small. A moment of rest you allowed without guilt. A compliment you absorbed without shrinking. A spontaneous gift, synchronicity, or sign of ease that you let in without needing to explain it. When you notice and name these moments, you're reinforcing the architecture of a new identity. The kind that receives as a default, not as an exception.

The practice of receiving also needs stillness. Not the kind of stillness that feels like absence or stagnation, but the kind that holds fertile ground. Sit for five minutes each day in silence with no purpose other than to notice your own energetic field. Feel into the places that are tense, skeptical, or resistant. You don't need to fix them. Just become aware of them, as if you're acknowledging someone who has been trying to protect you. Place your hand over your chest or your lower belly, wherever you feel sensation rise, and breathe there. Then say, softly and without force, "You don't have to guard this anymore." You're speaking to the old gatekeeper within your body. And slowly, day by day, it listens.

Sometimes the deepest receiving happens through pleasure. Not indulgence, but presence. Run your fingers through water and *feel* it. Sip something warm and actually taste it. Let music move through your chest instead of just your ears. These are not luxuries. They are calibration tools. They bring your body into now. And receiving only happens now. Not in the future you're trying to manifest, not in the memory of what you missed. Right here. In this inhale.

One of the most overlooked ways to practice receiving is to *ask for help*, and then actually accept it. Most people carry an unconscious vow of hyper-independence, forged in a time when help wasn't safe, or wasn't reliable. So they learn to do it all. And then wonder why nothing ever really flows in. Break the vow. Ask. Let someone support you, even if it's something simple. Let someone carry the groceries, offer insight, pay for the coffee, hold space while you speak. Your ability to receive wealth is mirrored in your ability to receive support without guilt. Without needing to "earn" it. Before you go to sleep, set the tone for your next day of receptivity. Place a hand on your body and speak a sentence that feels true and expansive. Something like, "I let go of control and open to more than I've ever allowed before." This isn't about belief. It's about rhythm. Repetition. Programming the frequency you want your field to hold when your conscious mind is quiet. This is how you train your channel to stay open even while you sleep. The more you practice, the more you'll notice your body soften in places it once hardened. Your voice will change. Your posture will shift. Your reactions to praise, money, time, ease, and support will start to feel less like flinches and more like natural breaths. That's the rewiring. Not through force. Through invitation. Through building a relationship with receiving that is gentle, daily, and undeniable. Not because you chased it down. But because you finally stopped pushing it away.

Chapter 8. Sacred Power vs. Performance

Why Action-Based Manifestation Keeps You Small

Most people don't manifest what they want. Not because they don't work hard enough, but because they work from the wrong layer of reality.

The modern mind is addicted to doing. It has been trained to believe that motion equals power. That to create something new, you must act your way into it. So the nervous system gets addicted to output, and the identity gets addicted to proving. Proving worth. Proving readiness. Proving capability.

But action rooted in unworthiness can never lead to abundance. Because the signal that gets sent is not "I am aligned." The signal is "I still need to earn it."

This is why so many people take all the right steps and still feel like they're running in circles. They attend the workshops, launch the projects, post the content, chase the next certification, and write down their goals every morning. But underneath the surface, the frequency is frantic. The field is filled with micro-signals of lack. And the body is exhausted.

The real blockage is not laziness. It's the *over-reliance on action as a form of control.* A subtle belief that unless you're moving, nothing is happening. That unless you push, nothing will arrive. This belief contracts your field. It teaches your system to grip rather than open. To perform rather than attract.

Manifestation isn't powered by performance. It's powered by coherence. Alignment. Wholeness.

When you are in energetic alignment, action becomes clean. It's not compulsive. It's not rushed. It doesn't come from fear of missing the window. It comes from a settled place in the body that says, "This is the next natural move." The action carries a different frequency. It doesn't try to *make* something happen. It *expresses* what's already been decided in the field.

This is the difference between force and command. Force relies on movement. Command relies on presence. And the deeper truth is that most of your manifestations are not waiting on action. They are waiting on congruence.

Congruence means that your identity, your energy, and your belief system are not in conflict. That your words match your nervous system. That your posture matches your expectation. That you are not affirming abundance while embodying scarcity in your tone, reactions, and schedule.

When your system is congruent, reality begins to respond before you lift a finger. You become magnetic without striving to be noticed. You become selected without pushing to be chosen. Things start happening that you didn't script. Invitations appear. Delays dissolve. Money arrives without explanation. This is not random. It is the natural consequence of frequency over force.

But because most people have been programmed in a productivity-obsessed world, they interpret stillness as laziness. They feel guilt when they're not busy. They fear that if they stop, they'll fall behind. This mental loop creates a distorted relationship with rest. It turns ease into a threat. So they keep acting, even when the signal is noisy. Even when their body says no. Even when nothing is flowing.

This is how the over-action paradigm shrinks your power. Not because action is wrong, but because it becomes your crutch. It becomes the thing you lean on instead of embodiment. Instead of clarity. Instead of frequency. You chase alignment through motion, when what you actually need is to *transmit* a different signal by becoming someone new.

Becoming someone new doesn't require a thousand micro-steps. It requires a frequency shift that your entire system recognizes as true. That shift can happen in an instant, but it only lasts when it's stabilized in the body. If the nervous system still feels unsafe with stillness, it will pull you back into action. Into proving. Into over-efforting. Not because it's right, but because it's familiar.

This is why some people meditate for years and still operate from a frequency of scarcity. Their actions are cloaked in spiritual language, but the underlying signal hasn't changed. They do rituals, but from obligation. They journal, but from fear of missing something. They say they trust, but their body tells a different story.

If the body is not included, there is no real shift.

Your body is your signal tower. It speaks before you do. It transmits before you post, apply, ask, or plan. This is why aligned receivers often appear "lucky" to others. They don't seem to be doing much, yet their lives fill with opportunities. But it's not luck. It's a clear, unwavering signal that says, "I am open. I am ready. I am not attached."

The paradox is that the less you act from scarcity, the more effective your aligned actions become. One clear move from congruence will create more results than a hundred frantic ones driven by fear. But to trust that, you have to detach from the cultural addiction to busyness. You have to stop defining your worth by your output.

If your identity is still fused with achievement, slowing down will feel like failure. You'll feel uncomfortable not "hustling." That discomfort is a detox. It's the old program breaking apart. Let it.

Power doesn't live in the doing. It lives in the being behind the doing. If your being is calibrated to trust, the field reorganizes. If your being is saturated in doubt, no amount of effort will override it.

To rewire this, you must start catching yourself in the subtle ways you seek proof. The refreshing of dashboards. The constant checking. The urge to say yes before checking in. The over-explaining. The pre-justifying. These are all micro-signals of misalignment. Not because they are wrong, but because they come from fear of not being enough without performance.

You are allowed to want overflow without burning out. You are allowed to be chosen without forcing visibility. You are allowed to rest and still be magnetic. But that requires a deep exhale from your system. A letting go of the identity that has earned everything by effort. A releasing of the part that says, "Unless I work hard, it's not mine."

That voice is not the truth. It's conditioning. Installed by systems that benefit from your exhaustion. It's time to uninstall it.

You do not have to abandon action. You only have to place it in right relationship with energy. When energy leads, action becomes sharp, clean, intentional. It no longer scrambles or grasps. It responds.

Let your nervous system feel what it's like to move from that place. Calm. Certain. Already full. From there, even the smallest step becomes a command to the field.

Stillness is not the absence of movement. It is the presence of power. And when you let that power take the lead, you stop chasing outcomes and start embodying inevitability.

Soft Power and Non-Linear Creation

Soft power is the invisible force that bends reality without strain. It's the frequency behind the smile that closes the deal before the pitch. The gaze that commands attention without a word. The presence that shifts a room's atmosphere simply by entering. You don't earn soft power by doing more. You cultivate it by becoming a clear signal — coherent, grounded, and unattached. It is the essence of non-linear creation: impact without force, movement without noise.

Most of the world is addicted to hard power. Strategies. Timelines. Linear projections. The idea that success is a staircase you must climb, step by step, sweating and proving your worth at each level. But soft power doesn't move in lines. It moves in spirals, in resonance, in quantum jumps. It doesn't ask, "What's the next task?" It asks, "What field am I inhabiting?" It doesn't obsess over visibility. It trusts its pull.

This doesn't mean you do nothing. It means what you do comes from a different place. You're not initiating action from lack, but from fullness. You're not chasing outcomes, but generating them internally first. You're not trying to convince the world of your value. You already know it — and the world reorganizes around that.

To understand soft power, you have to start noticing where you leak it. Every time you over-explain, you leak power. Every time you say yes to stay likable, you dilute your field. Every time you second-guess what you *know*, you confuse the signal. Soft power thrives on clarity, not performance. It doesn't need a stage. It needs congruence.

The world doesn't respond to your effort. It responds to your signal. And your signal becomes incoherent every time you split yourself. When your inner truth says "no" but your mouth says "yes," when your body feels tight but your mind pushes forward, when your instincts whisper "wait" but you override them to stay on schedule — those moments don't just create burnout. They collapse your field.

Soft power is a felt energy, not a tactic. You can't fake it, because it's not about how you *appear*. It's about how you *hold*. The body tells the truth. People feel the difference between someone rooted in their essence and someone performing a script.

Non-linear creation means you stop trying to push things forward on your timeline. You start listening to the timing of your field. Sometimes a single inner shift will create an avalanche of external change. Other times, a delay is the exact contraction needed to birth something truer. You stop asking, "Why is this taking so long?" and start asking, "What part of me hasn't fully aligned yet?"

Soft power tunes you into the subtle data that force misses. It's why some people create massive outcomes with little visible effort. They're not just lucky. They're attuned. They've learned to make decisions not from panic, but from inner coherence. They've stopped projecting their power onto algorithms, buyers, or gatekeepers. Instead, they become the source.

You don't need to fight for your place when you're the signal. You don't need to compete when you're creating in a field of your own. And you don't need to overwork to manifest when you've built a body that holds.

A body that holds is a body that doesn't chase. It doesn't need to stretch toward what's already on its way. It becomes a stable container for reality to reconfigure itself around. That level of magnetic stillness doesn't mean you are passive. It means you are precise. Your actions aren't compulsive. They are ceremonial. You do less, but you alter more. You speak less, but you penetrate deeper. You stop scattering your energy into proving, fixing, or seeking, and instead begin consolidating your field so that only what aligns can land.

This is where non-linear creation reveals its power. You start witnessing your outer world reorganize in response to subtle, internal adjustments. You withdraw energy from trying to control what isn't yours and redirect it into amplifying what is. The clarity of your signal becomes so strong that things begin arriving through improbable channels. Connections. Money. Solutions. Opportunities. They come not because you clawed at them, but because you cleared space for them to find you.

Soft power demands that you stop relying on confirmation from the external before believing in the internal. If you wait to feel worthy until the result shows up, you trap yourself in a cycle of reaction. But if you source the frequency first, and then move as if it's done, you become causality itself. You don't wait to be chosen. You become the chooser. This is what unhooks you from dependency and places you into authorship.

There's also a deep discipline in soft power. Not the rigid kind, but the sacred kind. The kind that trains your system to listen more deeply than your mind wants to. The kind that pauses before replying, that feels the difference between impulse and guidance, that refuses to act just to relieve discomfort. That level of presence becomes a spiritual practice. Not because it makes you good, but because it makes you clear.

The more coherent your inner field becomes, the faster reality bends around it. You no longer need to shove the boulder uphill. You simply step out of the misaligned pattern that was creating resistance in the first place. The terrain shifts when the traveler does. That's the secret most productivity paradigms miss. They optimize the path, but they never question the one walking it. They keep rearranging steps when what's needed is an identity that collapses the staircase entirely.

Let your daily decisions come from this place. Not "what should I do today," but "who am I when I do it." Ask before every move: is this aligned with the self who already has what I desire? Would she speak like this? Would she accept this opportunity? Would she chase this outcome or magnetize it? Would she distort herself to please, or would she sit in her silence and let the room adjust?

This is not about aesthetic softness. It's not about being gentle or quiet for the sake of it. It's about reclaiming the creative intelligence that doesn't need to be loud to be lethal. The power that doesn't run in straight lines. The path that doesn't require the same sacrifice to produce ten times the result. The feminine current that bends time by bending into truth.

When you embody soft power, your creations are no longer extensions of effort. They become expressions of essence. You no longer need to be louder, faster, or more productive to win. You only need to become a clearer channel for what wants to come through you. Creation begins to feel like breathing. Alive, effortless, precise. And from that place, what you build will hold. Because it was never forced into being. It was received.

Energetic Precision: Doing Less, Receiving More

There's a moment in every journey where the excess must be trimmed—not because you're lazy or giving up, but because you've grown too clear for waste. This is the point where doing more no longer multiplies your outcomes. It dilutes them. Where saying more weakens your impact. Where effort begins to betray essence.

Energetic precision is about directing your field with such clarity that the result doesn't depend on how hard you push but on how accurately you choose. It means no longer broadcasting mixed signals, leaking attention into things you don't want, or cluttering your manifestations with insecurity disguised as action. You stop trying to cover all bases and instead focus like a laser on the one move that alters the entire structure.

The overachiever archetype fears this. It equates busyness with worth. It wants to earn the right to receive by exhausting all available energy. But the field doesn't respond to how exhausted you are. It responds to how coherent you are. The less interference, the stronger the signal. The less you explain, justify, or defend, the more your desires take form.

So much of receiving is about restraint. Not repression, but sacred holding. Letting a desire exist without immediately attacking it with strategy. Letting it grow in your field until it becomes so normal that its arrival feels inevitable. This is the opposite of wishful thinking. It's energetic discipline. Every action you take, every thought you think, carries a frequency. Most people never audit that frequency. They do the right things on paper but with fragmented energy, so the result is either delayed, distorted, or denied. You cannot fake alignment. You can fake effort. You can fake confidence. But the field will always reflect the actual tone of your transmission, not the performance of it.

Energetic precision begins with a radical form of honesty. You start asking: where am I doing things I don't mean? Where am I saying yes when I mean no? Where am I giving from depletion instead of overflow? Where am I trying to manifest with my words but canceling it with my posture, my pacing, or my people-pleasing?

The body is a map of energy in motion. It always tells the truth before the mind catches up. If your jaw is tight, your shoulders tense, your breath shallow, your system is in contraction. If you're rushing, multitasking, overexplaining, you're not in precision. You're broadcasting confusion.

You're spreading your signal across too many channels, hoping one lands. But the field doesn't reward scattering. It rewards signal strength.

This is where you shift. You pause before you act. You get still before you speak. You stop asking what you *should* do and instead ask: what's the one move that holds the entire message?

Sometimes, it's a word. Sometimes, it's a boundary. Sometimes, it's no reply at all.

This is what magnetism is made of. Not noise, but clarity. Not force, but direction. The ability to say less and mean more. To do less and create more. Not because you're manipulating results, but because you've stopped leaking energy into everything you're not.

Your field sharpens as you remove the unnecessary. The apology, the overreach, the small talk that keeps your nervous system in false connection. Each of these moments is an energetic leak that says, *I don't fully trust my presence to speak for me.* And that's where you lose the transmission.

When you begin refining your output, you start noticing how many of your actions are survival-coded. Not generative. Not soul-chosen. Just legacy behaviors from a time you believed love was earned, or value was measured by sacrifice. And it isn't. Not anymore. You are allowed to choose something cleaner now. A frequency where the impact doesn't come from scale, but from congruence.

There is a moment in manifestation where adding more energy stops helping and starts scattering. When your nervous system is broadcasting urgency, the universe reads that as lack. The more you chase, the more it stretches away. Not as punishment, but because your field is out of sync with what you claim to be calling in. You say you want ease, but your body is in effort. You say you want overflow, but your daily pattern is contraction. Refinement is about walking your desire all the way down into your bones. It means calibrating your entire system to the tone of what you want to receive. If your goal is rooted in elegance, your actions cannot be frantic. If your vision is freedom, your process cannot feel like imprisonment.

Every time you move with precision, you're affirming that your desire already exists. You're not *making it happen*, you're meeting it halfway. Energetic coherence is the bridge.

To begin anchoring this in real time, start with your language. Speak slower. Say less. Eliminate the words that dilute your intent. You don't need disclaimers, just clarity. Let your tone carry the weight. Let the pauses do some of the work for you. That silence is not empty. It's dense with signal. Then move into your physicality. Your posture is part of your broadcast. How you stand, how you walk, how you look at someone when you speak. Your body can either reinforce your frequency or collapse it. You are either compressing your power into presence, or you are dissipating it through avoidance, fear, or nervous performance.

Next, examine your time. What are you filling it with that isn't necessary? What rituals, conversations, or obligations no longer serve your next level? Precision requires you to make cuts. You're not being cruel. You're creating space for what matters. Because you understand that receiving isn't about accumulation, it's about alignment.

You don't need more followers, more posts, more noise. You need more coherence. You don't need ten strategies. You need one decision that you back fully, with your voice, your energy, your silence, and your walk.

You become magnetic not by being everywhere, but by being fully here. In your body. In your word. In your knowing.

And from that place, you don't have to do more to have more. You simply have to stop contradicting what you've already claimed. You don't have to force an outcome. You let the field catch up to your frequency.

Energetic precision is not a tightening. It's a release. Of the fake effort. Of the noise. Of the idea that doing more proves you deserve more.

It's the discipline to stop when you've already said enough. The wisdom to trust when the signal has already been sent. The courage to hold the field without needing to fill the silence.

This is how you receive in overflow.

Not by running faster, but by becoming sharper.

Not by adding force, but by eliminating friction.

Not by chasing the timeline, but by stepping fully into the identity that time responds to.

Part III. Embodying the Portal

There comes a moment when you stop asking how to become the version of yourself you've glimpsed in visions, meditations, and quiet knowing. You stop chasing her as a future self and begin embodying her as the only self.
This is not a moment of learning. It is a moment of remembrance. Not of who you were told to be.
But of the one who always existed behind the layers you built to survive.
In this final phase, everything shifts from theory to cellular truth. The conversations you've had with possibility begin to root themselves into behavior. What once felt like magic becomes ordinary. What once required effort becomes identity. You're no longer manifesting from a script of effort or performance. You are becoming the script itself.
This part is not about adding more tools. It's about becoming the tool. Your body, your voice, your silence, your presence — each one becomes a transmission. Not of what you want, but of what you are. And that's the difference that collapses time.
Here, the work becomes quieter, deeper, and more precise. It's the calibration of your nervous system to your new frequency. It's the decision to let receiving be your default state. It's the ability to trust your magnetism so deeply that you no longer need to prove, push, or posture. You simply become a portal for what you already are.
In this part of the book, you'll be invited to practice what it means to live as the field, not separate from it. You'll step into the frequency of inevitability, not as a thought, but as a way of breathing. You'll dissolve the illusions that keep you looping and drop into the truth that already lives in your body.
No more seeking.
No more fixing.
No more waiting.
This is where you stop chasing portals and become the one everything flows through.

Chapter 9. The Architecture of Invisible Wealth

Thoughtforms, Belief Fields, and Emotional Command

Reality is not built solely on action, circumstance, or environment. It is constructed — and continually reconstructed — through the invisible architecture of energy: thoughtforms, belief fields, and the emotional signatures that animate them. These are not abstract spiritual theories. They are the unseen scaffolding shaping your choices, reactions, and manifestations. To ignore them is to live on the surface of your life. To command them is to become the architect of it.

A **thoughtform** is not just a passing idea. It's an energetic structure that holds shape. It is formed through repetition, attention, and emotional charge. The more you feed a thought — consciously or unconsciously — the more it becomes dense. Eventually, it begins to operate independently, like a small program running in the background of your mind, influencing perception, behavior, and even the signals you broadcast to others.

These structures do not disappear with affirmation alone. You cannot simply say "I am abundant" once and expect it to override a hardened thoughtform built through years of lack, fear, or financial trauma. The older and more emotionally reinforced a thoughtform is, the more weight it carries in your field. This is why some patterns feel impossible to break: they are not mental errors, they are energetic architectures.

Belief fields take this one step further. While thoughtforms are specific structures, belief fields are atmospheric. They form through the accumulation of many interconnected thoughts and experiences and operate like a filter — subtly distorting everything you perceive, expect, or accept as true.

Imagine two people walking into the same room. One holds a belief field of rejection. The other holds a belief field of welcome. The same neutral glance from a stranger will be read completely differently. One will brace. The other will soften. This has nothing to do with logic or facts. It has everything to do with the emotional command embedded in their belief field.

This is not about blame. You did not consciously choose every belief field you carry. Many were installed before you could question them — through family dynamics, early social conditioning, ancestral trauma, or cultural programming. Some belief fields don't even originate from you personally, yet they live in your system like inherited software, running silently, shaping your expectations of love, success, safety, or self-worth.

But the moment you become aware of these fields, you gain the ability to rewire them. And that rewiring does not begin with mental debate. It begins with **emotional command**.

Emotional command is not about suppressing feelings or pretending to be high-frequency. It is about recognizing that every emotion you embody becomes a transmitter. When you feel unworthy, you are not just thinking unworthy thoughts — you are radiating the signature of unworthiness into your field. That frequency becomes an instruction. Life organizes itself around that instruction.

The most magnetic people are not the ones who know the most. They are the ones who can hold emotional command over the energy they emit. Not through performance, but through embodied clarity. They don't spiral in self-doubt every time reality gives them feedback. They don't collapse when an outcome doesn't arrive on schedule. Their internal field remains anchored in a deeper truth — not because they've figured everything out, but because they've stopped negotiating with the old belief fields that used to run them.

True transformation happens not when you have more information, but when you hold a new frequency long enough for it to crystallize into your field. That takes presence, not performance.

The moment you stop outsourcing your emotional state to external conditions, you interrupt the old loop of dependency that kept the belief field alive. You are no longer waiting for reality to validate a new frequency. You are imprinting that frequency into reality. And because reality is not neutral, but responsive, it cannot help but rearrange around the new signal you carry.

This is why emotional command is not control. It is communion. You are not fighting your internal landscape into submission. You are choosing to regulate it in alignment with the reality you are creating. When fear arises, you meet it with presence, not panic. When doubt appears, you breathe instead of argue. These moments seem small, but they are the exact hinges on which timelines pivot. Your ability to hold a stable frequency when the old programming flares up is what determines whether you spiral back into the past or step into the field of the new.

Thoughtforms begin to dissolve not because you disprove them, but because you stop feeding them. When a thoughtform of scarcity whispers that you're behind, you recognize its voice and refuse to give it fuel. When a belief field of unworthiness tries to shrink your expansion, you don't fight it, you remain still in your truth until it exhausts its momentum. This is the deeper meaning of energetic sovereignty. You are no longer a sponge for inherited noise. You are an architect of the signal.

You may notice that as you stabilize in this new field, your nervous system also begins to re-pattern. The constant hypervigilance of scanning for threat, judgment, or rejection starts to quiet. Your body begins to feel safer in its own presence. This is not just energetic. It is deeply somatic. Thoughtforms are stored in the mind, but belief fields live in the body. If your body still braces every time you expand, the work is not to push harder, but to meet that bracing with presence until it no longer runs the show.

One of the most effective ways to shift belief fields is through repetition with feeling. Not robotic mantras, but clear, present declarations spoken from the body, not just the mouth. When you say, "I trust myself," feel your jaw, your spine, your stomach. Are they contracting or opening? Are you performing the sentence, or inhabiting it? This is how a new thought becomes more than a thought. It becomes a carrier wave for a new field.

The more consistently you inhabit this level of awareness, the more you start to notice how other people's belief fields operate as well. You become less entangled in projections, guilt loops, or emotional debt. You see that much of what people react to is not about you at all, but about the structures running their own system. You become less programmable. Less reactive. More precise.

Eventually, you find yourself moving through the world with a quiet clarity. You are not trying to convince reality of your worth. You are not negotiating with old scripts. You are simply holding a frequency with such integrity that the world must respond. This is not magic. It is mechanics. Reality, at its core, is obedient to command. And command begins with frequency.

No one can hold that frequency for you. No affirmation, no teacher, no strategy can override a field you continue to energize. But the moment you choose to shift your center of gravity — from thoughtform to intention, from belief field to energetic authorship — you collapse the false architecture and reclaim what was never actually lost: your command over what you feel, what you emit, and what you become.

Planting Codes Into Your Environment

Your environment is not neutral. It is a silent participant in your energetic field, constantly feeding your nervous system cues about who you are, what is possible, and how you are meant to feel. Most people unknowingly live inside spaces coded with stagnation, scarcity, guilt, or survival. Not because they chose those frequencies, but because they never intentionally planted new ones. If you don't code your environment, the old programs do it for you.

Every object, every corner, every repeated path in your home holds memory. That memory becomes feedback. You walk past the same mirror where you've judged yourself for years. You sit at the same desk where you've struggled to "figure it out." You open a drawer that holds items from a life that no longer fits. These moments may seem insignificant, but they are constantly reinforcing who you are allowed to be. Until you interrupt them.

To plant new codes, you begin by reclaiming your environment as a living system — one that can carry intention, memory, and instruction. This is not about decorating. This is about energetic authorship. You are not arranging space for aesthetics, but for activation.

Start small. Choose one object or one space that you interact with daily. A mirror. A candle. A teacup. Your front door. Before you even touch it, stand still in front of it. Close your eyes. Let your breath drop deeper. Feel what this object currently holds. Not with your mind, but with your body. Does it contract you or open you? Does it feel neutral, numbed, or already alive? Once you've read the energetic imprint, you begin the process of recoding. Let your body speak the frequency you want it to carry. You are not simply saying words at it. You are directing energy through voice, through breath, through intention. If it's a mirror, you might say, "Only recognition lives here now. Only clarity. Only truth." If it's a door, "This portal only opens to aligned timelines. Only expansion moves through." Speak it out loud, not for performance, but for impact. The sound itself becomes the carrier wave. Next, use your hands. Place them directly on the object or hold it in your palms. The skin has memory. The hands can seal commands. As you touch, visualize the object lighting up with the code you just installed. Imagine it pulsing with a frequency that is now non-negotiable. Let your body feel the shift. Don't rush this step. You're not just pretending. You're imprinting.

The shift is real when your body starts to respond to the object differently. When the mirror becomes a place of recognition instead of rejection. When your tea ritual becomes a ceremony of receiving instead of numbing. When your desk begins to feel like a command center, not a battlefield.

These codes can also be renewed. Just as we refresh our intentions in life, your space needs ongoing attunement. Over time, you'll notice which areas begin to dull again, where clutter accumulates, where energy feels sluggish. That is the cue to recode. Not with urgency, but with sovereignty. You are the architect of every cue your body receives. You can make those cues sacred.

One of the most overlooked but potent practices is the use of physical anchors — small objects intentionally charged to hold a specific energetic function. These can be stones, pieces of jewelry, handwritten notes, or even mundane items repurposed as living talismans. What matters is not the object's appearance, but your relationship to it. You're not assigning it meaning. You're giving it instruction.

When you give something instruction, you collapse ambiguity. That object no longer passively reflects your past or collective conditioning. It begins to obey your frequency. You are no longer surrounded by symbols of who you were. You are surrounded by collaborators in your becoming.

These charged objects serve as subtle pattern disruptors. You reach for a ring not just to wear it, but to step back into your intention. You light a candle not just for ambiance, but to reconnect with a version of you who no longer pleads, but commands. You place a handwritten sentence beneath your pillow, and each night your subconscious receives the same transmission: *I am allowed to receive.* These moments rewire your baseline not through pressure, but through repetition.

There is no need to force belief. The work is not about convincing your mind, but training your body to respond to new cues. As the space around you shifts, your nervous system begins to read it as safe to shift too. The mind will follow, not because it was argued into agreement, but because the field changed first. You feel different in the environment, and so different thoughts naturally emerge.

You can extend this practice to entire rooms. The room where you sleep. The place where you create. The door you walk through when returning home. Each of these becomes an initiation point when approached with awareness. You don't need to spend hours cleansing or over-ritualizing. What's needed is clarity of signal. You are not asking the space to change. You are instructing it to remember.

To refine the process further, pay attention to your sensory field. Scent, sound, texture, light — these are not frivolous details. They are gateways. A scent can carry the memory of a new timeline. A specific texture under your fingertips can mark the shift between your default identity and your chosen one. The way light enters the room in the morning can either trigger cortisol or invite reverence. Begin to notice how your body responds, not in theory, but in practice. If your jaw tightens every time you enter a certain room, don't just override it. Listen. What in that space needs to be uncoded, recoded, or removed?

There is also power in subtraction. Sometimes planting new codes means clearing the old ones. That drawer of expired paperwork, the clothes that no longer match your current self, the gifts you kept out of obligation but never resonated with — these are silent anchors to a version of you that is already obsolete. Letting them go is not a rejection of your past. It is an act of energetic honesty. If your field is crowded with residue, there is no room for the new to land.

You may begin to notice that your external reality starts to shift after recoding your space. Clients reach out. Conversations change tone. Resistance fades. This is not magic in the way we were taught to think of magic. It is physics. Your environment becomes coherent with your frequency, and coherence generates resonance. Life responds.

What you are building is not a better version of your current environment. You are constructing an energetic architecture that holds your becoming. A space that reminds you who you are when the world forgets. A space that interrupts fear, amplifies command, and holds your field steady when old patterns try to creep back in.

This is a form of leadership that few people ever consider. It is quiet. Invisible. And yet, it rewrites everything. Your home, your objects, your surroundings no longer carry static energy. They pulse with encoded clarity. And every time you move through them, you are not just living. You are landing deeper into the frequency of who you came here to be.

Ritualizing the Material World to Mirror Your Expansion

The material world is not a backdrop. It is a mirror. And if your outer world remains coded with scarcity, fragmentation, and over-efforting, it doesn't matter how many affirmations you whisper in the dark. Your environment will always pull you back into what it reflects.

To shift this, you must stop separating the spiritual from the tangible. Expansion is not just a mental game or an energetic feeling. It must be lived, embodied, and reflected in the physical choices you make each day. That means creating a material world that doesn't just look elevated, but holds your expansion like a ritual container.

Start by looking at how your current space speaks. Walk through your home not as its owner, but as its observer. What story does your kitchen tell about nourishment? What does your desk say about your relationship with time, purpose, or value? What signals are your clothes, your storage, your calendar sending to your nervous system?

This is not about aesthetics. You don't need to throw everything away or become minimalistic. You need to become intentional. The material world must be arranged in a way that stabilizes your next frequency, not your last one.

You can begin with micro-shifts. For example, your schedule. If you are filling every available moment with tasks, even healing tasks, even spiritual tasks, then your body is being taught to associate abundance with exhaustion. Begin inserting space, deliberately. A morning that begins with silence before stimulation. An evening that ends with presence, not performance. This is not self-care. This is reprogramming.

The same applies to your physical rituals. Brushing your hair, preparing your food, walking from one room to another — each of these is a portal. Most people rush through them unconsciously. But you can infuse them with intention, even if you say nothing out loud. The way you stir your tea. The way you open your curtains. The moment you step into the shower. These are not chores. They are scripts. And every action writes a line of code into your field.

One of the most underused practices is re-anchoring the identity through the body's daily rhythms. Ask yourself: what does the expanded version of me no longer tolerate? Not just mentally, but physically. Maybe it's eating standing up, answering messages before breathing in the morning, working under artificial light without pause. These small choices tell your subconscious who you are. When they shift, the self-concept does too.

You can then bring this into your space. Rearranging furniture is not about feng shui alone. It's about redirecting energy flow to support a new emotional landscape. If your workspace makes you feel boxed in, it may be anchoring a reality where effort equals struggle. If your bed faces the door and your sleep feels unsafe, your body might be holding on to hypervigilance. These are not superstitions. They are nervous system responses to architectural cues.

Let your space become ceremonial. Not stiff. Not precious. Alive. Every object, every corner, every sound becomes an opportunity to reinforce abundance or scarcity. When you reach for your journal, ask: is this where I collapse into looping thoughts, or where I declare vision? When you light a candle, ask: is this just ambiance, or is it marking a shift in consciousness?

What we're doing here is no longer separating "manifestation" from the ordinary. We're stitching it into everything. And the result isn't just a nicer home or better morning routine. It's a fully encoded life where even the unseen is given form — through the rituals you repeat, the spaces you design, and the behaviors you embody without needing to think about them. The nervous system doesn't speak English. It speaks sensation, rhythm, and repetition. So if your life feels like it keeps looping back into contraction, overwhelm, or lack, chances are your surroundings are wired to keep you there. This is not a flaw in your mindset. It is an echo in your field, reinforced by the physical patterns you've unconsciously allowed to stay.

Think of your home, your workspace, your car, your wallet, your phone background. All of these are interfaces. And just like software interfaces, they either accelerate the current you want to become or stall it. If every time you sit down to create, you are surrounded by clutter, your body prepares for chaos before you even begin. If your calendar is full of things that drain you, you are broadcasting the message: I have no room for what I say I want.

Energetic congruence is not found in wishing harder. It is built in the fabric of daily interaction. And the most powerful shifts are often the subtlest. The tea you pour becomes a moment to embody enoughness. The choice to place your phone outside the bedroom becomes a declaration that your frequency begins within you, not through a screen. The removal of broken or unused items signals to your subconscious that you no longer carry what doesn't work.

This is not about controlling your environment obsessively. It's about claiming your role as its architect. And when you begin to live as the artist of your space and schedule, you exit the identity of the survivor, the struggler, or the one waiting for permission. You become the signal. And that signal speaks louder than any affirmation ever could.

Start asking yourself one powerful question as you move through your day: *Does this reflect who I am becoming, or who I've already outgrown?* Let that question guide how you set the table, what you wear when no one is watching, how you design your week. The answers will come fast. And they won't require more effort. Only more honesty.

Sometimes this process will bring up grief. You may realize how long you've tolerated environments that dishonor your softness, your expansion, your truth. You may notice how long you've been performing inside a container that never felt like yours. That grief is sacred. It clears the ground for you to rebuild without compromise.

Do not rush to fill space once you clear it. The void is not a problem. It is the fertile soil. Let your new rituals emerge from desire, not discipline. Maybe you light incense before writing. Maybe you fold your clothes with intention. Maybe you wash your dishes as a sacred act of completion. What matters is not the action itself but the frequency you bring to it. These are your rituals of recalibration. And they create resonance that reality listens to.

The more attuned you become to this level of coding, the less effort it takes to hold your expansion. You no longer need to repeat mantras all day or fight for self-belief. Your space is holding it with you. Your schedule is reinforcing it. Your body is anchoring it. The outer is now working with the inner, not against it.

Eventually, this becomes your new normal. Your environment stops pulling you backward. It starts pulling you forward. And in that shift, manifestation is no longer something you try to do. It becomes the natural outcome of who you are being, moment by moment, in the world you've now shaped to carry your frequency.

That is when the material world stops being an obstacle. It becomes the mirror of your expansion. And every surface, every rhythm, every choice becomes a sacred yes to the version of you who no longer waits to become. She already is. And the world around her reflects it, effortlessly.

Chapter 10. Frequency Conflict and Subconscious Sabotage

Recognizing Inner Conflicts Between Safety and Desire

There's a specific type of split that quietly hijacks your ability to receive what you say you want. It's the fracture between your conscious desires and the parts of you that do not feel safe having them.

You might say you want abundance, visibility, intimacy, or freedom. And you may even be taking aligned action. But if another part of you equates those outcomes with danger, exposure, judgment, loss, or rejection, the result is energetic static. You oscillate between calling something in and subconsciously pushing it away. And because this happens at a deep, often invisible level, it can feel like you're hitting a wall without knowing why.

This inner war is not self-sabotage in the way we've been taught to think of it. It's not laziness or fear of success. It's a protective mechanism. A part of you learned, often early in life, that getting what you want might come at a cost. So instead of allowing the expansion, your system prioritizes survival. Not because you're broken. But because your body remembers.

Desire without safety is like pressing the gas and brake at the same time. You burn out without ever moving forward. That's why willpower isn't enough. That's why strategy alone won't break the cycle. What's needed is not more effort but integration.

Begin with deep listening. Take one of your biggest desires and sit with it quietly. Ask: *What would actually happen if I had this now?* Let the answer come from your body, not your mind. Notice where you feel tightness, contraction, or hesitation. That's not resistance to the desire. It's a signal from a part of you that's afraid.

Now ask that part a second question: *What are you afraid this will cost me?* You might hear answers like: "People will leave," "I'll be judged," "It will all disappear," or "I won't be able to handle it." These are not irrational fears. They are echoes of past moments where expansion felt unsafe, where being seen led to punishment, or where having more meant losing connection.

By surfacing these fears instead of suppressing them, you shift from inner opposition to inner conversation. You stop shaming the part of you that is afraid and begin reparenting it with presence. The body does not shift through logic. It shifts through felt safety.

To resolve the split, create rituals of safety around the thing you want. If your body believes that more money means more pressure, start associating money with support instead. If love feels like abandonment, build new relational patterns where presence is consistent and regulated. If visibility triggers fear of attack, slowly increase your exposure while anchoring into self-trust and containment.

This doesn't mean you wait to act until every part of you feels ready. It means you bring those parts with you, rather than dragging them behind. You acknowledge that your system is layered, and each layer deserves to be heard. When all parts are moving in the same direction, manifestation becomes less about force and more about allowance.

There is a practice that helps illuminate these splits with clarity, and it's called **Desire-Safety Mapping**. This is a somatic journaling tool designed to bring unconscious contractions into conscious awareness, so you can work with them instead of against them.

Let's walk through it step by step. Grab a pen and paper, and choose a single desire that feels important right now. Something that feels just out of reach, or something you've been chasing without results. Write it at the top of the page. Then beneath the written desire on your page, draw two columns. Label one **Desire** and the other **Danger**.

Under **Desire**, write out the core outcomes you associate with having this thing. Go deep. If your desire is financial abundance, go beyond "more money." Ask yourself, what would this really give you? Freedom? Relief? Recognition? A new identity?

Now, under **Danger**, let yourself write freely without censoring. What would this same outcome *threaten*? What could go wrong if you received this? Who might feel threatened? What old identity would no longer fit? What level of responsibility might you not feel prepared to hold? Be honest, even if it feels uncomfortable.

You're not trying to dismantle your desire. You're locating the invisible weight beneath it. You're seeing how your own nervous system has been trained to equate expansion with exposure, wealth with abandonment, love with betrayal, or success with failure. These contradictions don't cancel out your desire, but they do slow or splinter the energy behind it.

Next, circle the fear statements that feel most emotionally charged. Take a breath and read each one out loud. Notice what it evokes. Where do you feel it in your body? What memories does it pull up? This is the part of you that needs safety to come along for the ride.

Instead of forcing or overriding, imagine holding this fear gently. Speak to it directly, with the voice of the version of you who *has* already embodied the desire. Tell this part: "You're allowed to be afraid. But I'm not going to leave you behind." Let that promise land.

Sometimes the most powerful reprogramming is not shouting affirmations but whispering permission. Not forcing belief but offering safety. You are the container. You decide how the energy moves. And when safety and desire unify, the signal you emit becomes clean. There's no static, no conflict, no retraction. What you ask for can find you because nothing inside you is pushing it away.

To deepen the integration, you can create a micro-ritual where you symbolically unite the part that desires and the part that fears. Write a letter from your desiring self to your protective self. Let her express what she truly wants, what she's ready to claim, what she's tired of waiting for. Then switch roles, and write a response from the protective self. Let her express her fears, her role, her loyalty, her need to keep you safe. Finally, write a third message from your integrated self — the one who can hold both. This voice is the key. It creates space where nothing has to be exiled.

When you live from this integrated place, your manifestations become more consistent, and your desires feel less heavy. You don't have to convince yourself or trick your body into cooperating. You're no longer trying to outrun fear. You're walking with it, holding its hand, reminding it that you're not where you used to be.

And that's the secret. Manifestation isn't just about projecting into the future. It's about resolving what's fragmented in the now. When the channel between safety and desire is open, your energy becomes congruent. You no longer signal yes and no at the same time. You become a coherent field. And that coherence is what pulls reality into alignment.

Your system will always move toward safety. So make expansion feel safe. Make love feel safe. Make wealth feel safe. Not by pretending you're fearless, but by anchoring into the kind of inner safety that holds your desire without flinching. That is the foundation of all sustainable creation. That is what allows you to want more, receive more, and hold more — without collapse.

Frequency Splitting: How You Cancel Out Your Own Power

You can have the right vision, the right rituals, and the right words — but if your energy is split, none of it will land.

Frequency splitting is not just a mindset issue. It's an energetic contradiction where two opposing signals are being broadcast at once. On the surface, you may be speaking powerfully, visualizing clearly, even taking aligned action. But underneath, another frequency is running — one made of doubt, resentment, fear, or unworthiness. And that second frequency doesn't just dilute the first. It cancels it.

This is why things stall. Why opportunities don't land. Why the moment you get close to something good, it slips or unravels. It's not that you're doing something wrong. It's that you're leaking signal.

Every desire is a frequency. And that frequency must be held consistently for reality to rearrange around it. But holding it requires congruence. When your internal field is broadcasting two different emotional truths — one rooted in desire, the other in fear — the quantum field doesn't respond to the louder one. It responds to the one you *believe* more deeply.

Take a simple example. You say, "I want to be fully seen," and on the surface that feels true. But if a deeper layer of your nervous system still associates visibility with danger, rejection, or past trauma, your field is sending out a secondary broadcast: "Visibility is not safe." The result is energetic short-circuiting. Mixed messages. Manifestation delay.

This is not about blame. It's about awareness. Because the moment you recognize the split, you can begin to unify it.

Let's go deeper. Think about times when you've made a bold decision — to start a business, leave a relationship, move toward your next level. You felt clarity. Forward motion. Power. But within days or hours, you began to question it. Was it too risky? Was it too fast? Did you make a mistake? That's a frequency split. And the danger isn't the doubt itself. The danger is when the doubt becomes habitual. When your field starts cycling between "Yes" and "No" so quickly that it generates static instead of signal.

Static repels outcomes. It creates interference that blocks clarity, guidance, and magnetism. You might still receive things, but they come with friction, delay, or collapse. And the pattern repeats.

There's a hidden reason this happens: control. Splitting your frequency gives you the illusion of safety. If one part of you reaches and another part retracts, you're never fully exposed. You get to *try* without truly risking. You get to *want* without fully opening. You stay in the space of effort, without surrender. But effort doesn't move the field. Coherence does.

Coherence means your thoughts, emotions, intentions, and actions are aligned. They're not arguing with each other. They're not negotiating behind the scenes. When you become coherent, your energy stops seeking reassurance and begins to radiate certainty. Not because you know the outcome, but because you've made a full decision.

This is where most people stall. They say they've chosen, but their field is still in negotiation. One hand is on the door, the other is reaching for the window. One voice is asking for more, another is whispering that it's too much. That's the split. And until it resolves, the desire stays in limbo.

The split is subtle at first. You'll feel it as a tension in the body, a pull behind the ribs, a slight contraction when you speak your desire out loud. You'll notice it when you try to move forward and immediately feel the need to shrink, to justify, to backpedal just enough to not be too much.

This is not about overcorrecting or suppressing doubt. It's about integrating the part of you that's afraid so that it no longer broadcasts a separate message. That part is not wrong. It's protecting you from pain you once didn't know how to process. But protection and expansion require different postures. One contracts, one opens. Both can't lead.

To detect the split, speak your desire aloud and then immediately get quiet. Not mentally quiet, but physically. Breathe. Feel. Ask: is there friction? Is there a part of me that flinches, that doesn't believe I can have this, or that feels shame for even asking?

That's the first signal. From there, the work is not to force that part into silence, but to meet it with presence. To say, "I hear you, but I'm leading now." Emotional command doesn't mean force. It means choosing which frequency is allowed to set the tone. When you choose consciously, the noise begins to settle. The distortion clears. The field becomes coherent again.

Power returns the moment you take responsibility for your signal. Not responsibility in a punishing or perfectionist way, but as a reclamation of authorship. When your field stops negotiating, your life stops negotiating with you. People respond differently. Opportunities stabilize. The things you used to chase start to arrive without push. Because now, you are transmitting a unified, consistent, unmistakable truth.

Most people live in a loop of unconscious frequency splitting. They ask for change while anchoring themselves to sameness. They pray for abundance while fearing visibility. They want intimacy while resenting dependence. And they can't understand why nothing sticks. It's not a punishment. It's just misalignment between the stated desire and the embodied broadcast.

The only way to resolve that is through energetic congruence. Words are not enough. Vision boards are not enough. You must become the frequency of what you want. That means no more rehearsing the fear version. No more indulging the split when it tries to fragment you. You bring your field into order by refusing to collapse into contradiction.

Sometimes this takes time. Sometimes the nervous system needs reconditioning before it feels safe to hold the higher signal. But it's never out of reach. Each moment offers a choice point: amplify the old pattern, or stabilize the new one. This is why consistency matters. Not for hustle. Not for grind. But because consistency creates coherence, and coherence is magnetic.

As you move through your day, begin to notice the signals you send in small moments. Do you speak abundance while scanning for lack? Do you ask for love while preparing to be let down? Do you commit to growth while secretly waiting for the fall? These micro-signals matter. They shape the field. They tell the unseen world what you truly expect.

You are always manifesting, not just with your intentions but with your contradictions. Every hesitation, every unprocessed fear, every unconscious pull toward safety tells the field to hold back. When you clean up the split, there is no more confusion. The energy around you becomes unmistakably clear. You are ready. You are aligned. You are undivided.

And when you are undivided, the field has no choice but to respond. Not eventually. Not someday. But now.

Integration Practices for Signal Coherence

When desire and safety live in conflict, the body sends mixed messages. One part wants to expand, to receive more, to step into visibility or wealth or intimacy. Another part, usually quieter but more constant, tightens at the thought. Not because it doesn't want the desire, but because it doesn't trust what it means. More can feel like exposure. Change can feel like risk. Receiving can feel like loss of control. These silent undercurrents are what fracture your signal.

To manifest in full, you don't just need a strong desire. You need an undivided field. That means your inner world and outer behavior broadcast the same thing, consistently. The tone of your nervous system matches the tone of your voice. The energy behind your rituals aligns with the energy behind your choices. And your body trusts that what you're calling in is not only wanted, but safe.

This is what we call *signal coherence* — the alignment of thought, emotion, nervous system state, and action into one continuous frequency. When your signal is coherent, your life becomes responsive. You stop living in delay. You stop attracting mirrors of your doubts. You stop confusing the field with half-yeses and hesitant no's. Reality becomes clear and simple again. It reflects what you are, not what you're trying to pretend.

So how do we achieve that coherence when the split between desire and safety has become patterned into the body?

You don't force your way there. You integrate.

Integration isn't about overriding the part of you that's afraid. It's about creating space where both desire and safety can coexist. Where your body can learn that more is not a threat. That expansion does not require betrayal. That visibility does not mean abandonment. Integration means meeting the fear without feeding it. You allow it, feel it, speak to it — and still move forward.

A simple and powerful practice for integration begins with presence. Not mental awareness, but full-body presence. Choose a desire that you feel both drawn to and slightly scared of. Say it out loud. Feel the sensation that arises. It might be heat in the chest, tightness in the belly, or a pulling behind the throat. Don't analyze it. Just stay with it. Breathe into the exact place the body contracts.

Then speak directly to that part of your body. Imagine it has a voice. What is it afraid of? What does it need in order to feel safe while this desire comes in?

Most of the time, it will not ask you to abandon the desire. It will ask you to move slower. To stay grounded. To not leave yourself. That's all it wants — to know you'll still be here, inside your body, as the new thing arrives.

Once you've named the fear and acknowledged its signal, you can begin to update the emotional association tied to the desire. This is where most people stop. They feel the fear and assume it means "not now." But what if fear is not a stop sign, but a doorway? What if it's the part of you that's been waiting to be included in the future you're building?

This is the shift. Not from fear to fearlessness, but from fragmentation to wholeness.

Let the desire stay. Let the fear speak. Then bring them both into the same breath. Breathe in the desire. Breathe out the tension. Again and again. Until the body learns that both can live here.

Once the body begins to feel that it is allowed to hold both ends of the spectrum, integration deepens. You become a safe space for your own bigness. The parts of you that used to panic at change start relaxing into trust. You stop disqualifying your desires in subtle ways. You stop asking for one thing with your words and canceling it out with your frequency.

This is where subtle rituals can anchor the shift.

Your body responds to repetition. It reads your daily choices as instructions. You don't need to force a new belief. You only need to signal it consistently. That could mean lighting a candle while saying your desire out loud each morning, while placing a hand on the part of your body that once tightened against it. It could mean choosing clothes, sounds, or scents that carry the signal of what you're stepping into. The body starts to pair the new with pleasure, not pressure. It stops bracing. It starts allowing.

Coherence doesn't come from having no fear. It comes from not hiding it. When fear is acknowledged, it becomes a collaborator, not a saboteur. The nervous system stops resisting and starts softening. And that softening is where the transmission changes.

You will notice when your signal is no longer split. Life stops testing you in the same way. You stop receiving half-yeses from the world because you're no longer sending half-signals. People feel something different in your presence, even if they can't explain it. You are congruent. And congruence has a gravitational pull.

There is a moment in the integration process when you realize you're no longer afraid of your own power. You don't flinch when something comes easily. You don't rush to sabotage what flows. You don't assume loss is around the corner. You stop making yourself pay for receiving.

This is the evidence that the channel is clear. That your body is no longer operating on outdated commands. That safety and desire have stopped fighting for dominance and started walking in the same direction.

To maintain this, you don't need to be perfect. You need to be honest. Keep listening. Keep responding. Let your system recalibrate as often as needed. You may have to re-meet the fear every time you expand. That's not failure. That's evolution. Integration is not a one-time event. It is a rhythm, a relationship, a return to coherence again and again.

Sometimes, what blocks your signal is not what you believe, but what you never dared to feel. Emotions you buried in order to function. Grief that never had a witness. Rage you swallowed to stay agreeable. These unprocessed feelings are the static in the field. They distort your ask without you realizing. Clearing them is not about purging. It's about presence. Letting the emotion finally have its place so that your desire doesn't have to carry it anymore.

When the internal terrain is clean, your signal doesn't just reach further. It hits deeper. You stop attracting scattered opportunities and start drawing in matches that recognize you immediately. You don't have to chase what belongs. You become the resonance that calls it in.

Coherence is not about being high vibe. It's about being whole. Every part of you gets to belong. And when that belonging happens on the inside, reality responds in kind.

That's when manifestation stops being something you try to do. It becomes the inevitable reflection of who you've become. You are no longer the one broadcasting a desire you secretly doubt. You are the one whose signal is clear, true, and fully received.

And when that happens, the field answers. Every time.

Chapter 11. The Gateway of Sacred Rebellion

Burning the Scripts That Kept You Small

There are stories inside you that were never yours to begin with.

You inherited them in moments of fear, silence, rejection, or obedience. Scripts written by someone else's voice, enforced by someone else's belief, anchored in someone else's survival. They live in the subtle phrases that loop inside your head: *"I'm too much," "I don't want to make anyone uncomfortable," "I have to prove I deserve this,"* or *"It's safer to stay small than to risk being seen."* These sentences are not thoughts. They are programs. Installed, repeated, reinforced. And every time you act according to them, you fortify their grip.

To step into what's truly yours, you don't just need to dream bigger. You need to burn what no longer fits.

This is not metaphorical. The body responds to symbols, not theory. What lives in the subconscious is moved through energy, sensation, and ritual. That's why you need a moment—an act—that tells your system the old rules no longer apply. That the version of you who agreed to them has ended. That a new frequency is now in command.

The ritual of burning is ancient. Across cultures, fire has always been used to transmute, to purify, to release what the body can't hold anymore. Fire doesn't ask questions. It transforms. It doesn't need permission. It simply does what it's made to do.

You can use this force deliberately, with precision and clarity, to signal the end of a pattern.

Start by identifying the script. Not the general story, but the precise sentence that controls your behavior. You'll know it because it feels like a loop. It returns in moments of vulnerability or visibility. It shows up before expansion. It sounds like protection, but it feels like contraction. Write it down. One line per sheet. Keep it short. No justifying, no analyzing. Just the raw sentence, as it appears in your body.

Examples might be:

- "If I shine too much, I'll be punished."
- "Receiving comes with a price."

- "They'll only love me if I stay useful."
- "Power is dangerous."

Once you've written down the exact lines, pause. Read them out loud. Notice the parts of your body that tighten, shrink, or go numb. These scripts are not just ideas. They are somatic instructions. They've been living in your nervous system, shaping your posture, your tone, your patterns of giving and withholding.

Now, it's time to prepare for the burn.

Create a safe space—somewhere you can be fully present, uninterrupted, and undisturbed. If fire is not physically available, use a symbolic container: a bowl of water, a candle, a shredder, or even a digital ritual where you erase the words with intention. But if you can, use real flame. The primal element speaks directly to the subconscious.

This is not about destruction. This is about release. You are not killing a part of yourself. You are liberating the part of you that's been trapped inside someone else's idea of who you should be.

Before burning each script, read it one last time. Then speak a phrase of release. Choose words that feel true in your system. For example:

"I no longer carry this."

"This was never mine to begin with."

"I return this to where it came from."

"This no longer runs my life."

Say the words, then burn the page.

Let the smoke carry the old agreement away.

Let the ashes be proof of your choice.

Let the fire show your body that something irreversible just occurred.

As each page disappears into flame, a subtle shift begins. Not always loud. Sometimes it's just the absence of tension where it used to live. Sometimes it's a tear you didn't expect, a breath you didn't know you were holding, a sudden clarity that slices through the noise. What you're feeling is spaciousness. The old script was occupying energetic territory. Now that space is open, and your system needs something to inhabit it with intention. This is where most people stop short. They release, but they don't rewire. And an unoccupied space, left unchecked, often becomes fertile ground for the same story to sneak back in under a new disguise. You need to install something new. Not to control it, but to anchor the version of you that no longer submits to the outdated script.

This doesn't mean inserting fake affirmations you don't believe. It means choosing one single sentence that feels true, even if only one percent of you believes it. That's all you need. One percent is enough to start a new frequency.

The most powerful replacement sentences aren't grand declarations. They are subtle recalibrations of inner authority. For example:

"I am allowed to take up space."

"It is safe for me to be seen."

"Receiving is my natural state."

"I belong where my energy flows with ease."

Speak your new sentence out loud. Slowly. Let the sound of your own voice imprint it into your field. Repeat it until it settles. Not like a chant, but like a vow. A private agreement between you and the self that is ready to lead. Then look around.

Notice how your physical space still carries remnants of the old story. Objects, routines, digital trails, even clothing can echo the outdated script. You don't need to purge everything at once. But begin to walk through your world with the eyes of someone who no longer submits to smallness. What would you stop tolerating? What would you rearrange? What would you stop explaining?

The ritual doesn't end with the fire. It continues in the way you move, respond, and choose from this moment forward. Every time you say yes to what expands you, you reinforce the new script. Every time you pause instead of shrinking, you carve a deeper path for this version of you to take root. There is no need to be perfect. What matters is precision and presence.

Some people feel a kind of energetic detox after burning the old scripts. Old emotions rise, dreams intensify, fatigue shows up as the body recalibrates. This is natural. You just unplugged from a long-held source of tension. Let your system adjust. Drink water. Sleep more. Be quiet with yourself. Let the space remain empty for a moment before rushing to fill it. That emptiness is intelligence. It is re-patterning you.

And most importantly, don't wait for proof before trusting the shift. You are the proof. The ritual was not symbolic. It was functional. Something changed. It may show up quietly, or in waves. But your field heard the command. Your subconscious got the message. And life will now begin to reflect it, sometimes in ways that surprise you.

You don't need to hustle for worth anymore.

You don't need to be a mirror for other people's comfort.

You are not here to survive someone else's programming.

You are here to create in alignment with the self that was buried underneath the noise.

Now that the script is ash, only one question remains:

What do you choose to write in its place?

Crafting Your Own Metrics of Overflow

You've been told what success looks like. Numbers in a bank account. Square footage. Milestones reached. Followers counted. But these metrics were never neutral. They were designed inside a system that profits from your chronic dissatisfaction. They feed on the gap between where you are and where you've been taught you should be. And the more you chase someone else's definition of "enough," the more disconnected you become from your own internal compass.

The truth is that overflow isn't a number. It's a state. And until you define it for yourself, you'll always be vulnerable to chasing illusions. You'll keep pushing for more without ever landing in the feeling you thought more would bring.

This is the first rupture to repair. Not how much you have, but how you measure what truly nourishes you. You must craft metrics that reflect your values, not the culture's expectations. You must learn to track your life through the lens of resonance, not performance.

Start by asking the real question: What does *abundance* feel like in my body? For some, it's ease. Spaciousness. Time without rush. For others, it's depth. Real presence in a conversation, a meal, a moment. Sometimes it's sovereignty, the ability to choose how your energy moves without being at the mercy of external pressure.

Now compare that to the version of success you've been conditioned to pursue. Is that version delivering any of those feelings? Or has it become a performance loop where value is always just out of reach?

This isn't about abandoning ambition. It's about uncoupling your value from extraction. It's about redefining "enough" in a way that allows your nervous system to rest without collapsing your vision. You can desire more while still being in a state of overflow. But only when your internal metrics lead the way.

To get there, you must be willing to track your life differently.

Instead of defaulting to how much you earned or accomplished this week, ask:

- How often did I feel connected to myself?
- Where did I experience beauty, even if fleeting?
- Did I honor my energy cycles, or override them?

- What did I choose from alignment, not pressure?
- Did I say no from wholeness?

These questions aren't soft. They are fierce. Because they reclaim the measurement of value from systems that want to keep you endlessly chasing.

Your metrics of overflow might be entirely unrecognizable to others. Maybe it's a daily bath uninterrupted. Maybe it's spacious mornings without phone notifications. Maybe it's meals eaten slowly, rituals kept sacred, a certain quality of softness returned to your body. Maybe it's how deeply you listen before speaking. Or how much of your time is spent in resonance rather than reactivity.

Let yourself be unreasonable about what matters to you. Let it contradict productivity culture. Let it offend the versions of yourself that were raised on achievement-as-survival. You are not here to prove your worth through exhaustion. You are here to live by design, not demand.

And in order to do that, you need a way to recognize when you've entered overflow, so you can stabilize it. Not wait for the next breakdown to reassess, but live in an ongoing state of course correction, alignment, and self-authority.

Crafting your own metrics is not a conceptual act. It's a full-body recalibration. It asks you to name what matters, live by it daily, and allow it to determine your pace, your boundaries, and your choices.

A powerful way to integrate your own definition of overflow into daily life is to ritualize your tracking. Not as a performance or a checkbox, but as a sacred conversation with your own energy. This means regularly asking, *Where am I aligned, and where have I betrayed myself in the name of staying on schedule or appearing successful?*

Set aside a few minutes at the end of the day to tune in. Not to analyze, but to feel. What choices expanded you? Which ones contracted you? Where did your body soften, your breath slow, your heart open? These are not vague sensations. They are data points in your unique energetic language. The more often you pause to notice them, the more fluent you become in reading your real metrics.

One of the simplest ways to bring this to life is to choose three internal markers of overflow that matter to you. They must be felt, not just observed. For example, you might choose:

- A sense of grounded presence
- Spacious time to tend to your body and inner world
- Connection to meaning and beauty in your surroundings

Write these down. Post them somewhere visible. Let them interrupt the trance of productivity. When you start measuring your days through these markers, your nervous system begins to rewire. The absence of constant striving no longer signals failure. Instead, it begins to register safety in the state of sufficiency.

This is the reversal that changes everything.

When you operate from your own internal measures of overflow, you stop outsourcing your identity to outcomes. You are no longer waiting for proof that you've "made it." You begin to move as someone who already carries the quality of life they once thought they needed external validation to claim. That state magnetizes experiences that reflect it, not because you're chasing them, but because you're attuned to receive them.

This internal anchoring also clarifies your decisions. You no longer pursue opportunities just because they look impressive. You feel into whether they match your metrics. Whether they honor your rhythms. Whether they align with the world you're building, not the one you're trying to leave behind.

This shift may cause friction. People around you might not understand why you say no to things that once excited you. You might feel guilt when resting or grief when letting go of identities built on proving. That's part of the recalibration. It's not a sign you're wrong. It's a sign you're crossing the threshold between externally driven ambition and internally guided overflow.

If you stay with this process long enough, you'll find something remarkable. What you once thought would require force begins to arrive through clarity. Desire that used to feel distant becomes embodied. You begin to notice the elegance of aligned timing. You meet people who speak the language you've just learned to articulate. Opportunities show up not because you hunted them down, but because your presence became unmistakably coherent.

This is not magic thinking. It's the natural result of living from the inside out. The moment you stop chasing metrics designed to keep you disempowered, you reclaim the authority to define and embody your own definition of wealth, success, and impact.

Let this become your ongoing practice. Not a one-time reframe, but a living, breathing relationship with yourself. Let your metrics evolve with you. As your capacity expands, so will your understanding of what overflow looks like in this season. And as you keep aligning your life around what is true for you, the external world will slowly begin to reflect the internal abundance you've chosen to prioritize. Not as a performance. But as a quiet, radiant, and unshakeable way of being.

Rebellion as Activation, Not Resistance

Rebellion has long been misunderstood. It's been painted as loud, reactive, oppositional. A middle finger to the system. A breaking of rules for the sake of defiance. But real rebellion—the kind that changes lives at the cellular level—is not about pushing against. It's about turning toward. Toward what's true. Toward what's been buried. Toward the version of you that was never allowed to exist fully within the systems you were taught to obey.

This kind of rebellion is not a tantrum. It's an initiation.

When your life begins to feel like it's running on someone else's script, when you feel trapped by rules you never consciously agreed to, when you notice yourself following patterns that numb instead of nourish—you are being invited into rebellion. Not as escape. But as activation.

This activation does not need to be dramatic. It does not require destruction. It begins in a much quieter place: where you notice the lie and decide not to carry it anymore. Where you feel the weight of performing for safety and choose instead to anchor into something deeper. Where you stop waiting for permission to become who you already are.

That is sacred rebellion. Not fueled by resentment, but by alignment.

You're not here to resist the old system with your entire nervous system clenched and your breath held. You're here to unplug from it. To stop feeding it your energy. To stop making it the reference point for who you get to be. Rebellion, in this form, is a sovereign act of remembering. It says: "I no longer agree to play this role just to be accepted. I remember what I am. And I'll build my life around that."

This can look like saying no to a pathway that would have earned praise but cost you your presence. It can look like prioritizing slowness in a culture addicted to speed. It can look like designing your days around beauty, sensation, and clarity instead of pressure, performance, and external validation.

In these choices, rebellion stops being a reaction to authority and becomes an expression of authority.

When you see rebellion through this lens, you stop needing something to fight. You no longer define yourself by what you're pushing against. You define yourself by what you're willing to embody without apology. This is what makes it usable. You don't need to wait for the next injustice or disappointment to trigger your awakening. You get to choose it now.

And you make it practical by asking one simple question: *Where in my life am I still negotiating my truth in exchange for safety or belonging?*

Where are you holding your breath instead of speaking? Where are you working for a version of success you don't even resonate with? Where are you performing resilience instead of honoring what's real?

These are not rhetorical questions. They are entry points. Because once you identify the negotiation, you can stop making it. Once you recognize the place where you've been quieting your signal, you can reclaim it.

This kind of rebellion will not be applauded. It won't come with instant rewards. It might make people uncomfortable. But it will restore your frequency. And from there, you begin to create—not just react.

You'll notice the difference in how you move. You'll stop trying to be louder than the noise, and instead, become so attuned to your signal that the noise becomes irrelevant. You'll stop debating your worth with systems that benefit from your doubt, and start designing an inner world where your value is never up for discussion.

That's the threshold. And we're about to step into what happens when you cross it.

Once your signal is intact, you no longer crave validation from systems you've outgrown. You don't need to convince, perform, or explain. You're not arguing for your value anymore. You're simply living it. And that's where rebellion becomes power. Not through force, but through the quiet, consistent refusal to abandon yourself.

You begin to create a different kind of friction—not one rooted in opposition, but one that naturally disrupts what cannot hold your frequency. Relationships shift. Opportunities filter. Environments rearrange. Not because you're pushing anything away, but because you're no longer adjusting yourself to match what keeps you small. Your presence alone becomes a sorting mechanism.

This is why rebellion, in its sacred form, requires capacity. Not just emotional bravery, but energetic stability. Because the more aligned you become, the more you will be asked to hold the dissonance between your truth and the world that was built to suppress it. You will feel it in conversations where your clarity unsettles someone still performing. You will feel it in rooms where your authenticity feels louder than anyone else's words. You will feel it in moments when your refusal to betray yourself costs you approval or opportunity.

But you'll also feel something else. Something deeper. Something steady. A sense that you are no longer living a double life. That your inner world is no longer hidden behind performance or diluted by compromise. That you can finally hear yourself clearly, and that what you hear is worth building around. The nervous system, over time, adapts to this new standard. At first, it may feel like risk. It may interpret your authenticity as danger, simply because it isn't familiar. But rebellion, practiced consistently, becomes safety. Not the kind sold to you by external structures, but the kind built through congruence. The safety of knowing you're not abandoning your own knowing to be accepted. The safety of honoring your desire instead of diluting it. The safety of walking into a room already anchored in who you are.

This is the foundation of sovereign manifestation. You cannot manifest fully from a self that is still negotiating its right to exist. You cannot co-create with life if you're pretending to be someone else to survive it. You have to let rebellion clean the channel. You have to let it remove the static of people-pleasing, the noise of overthinking, the distortions of inherited fear. Rebellion does not destroy who you are. It destroys what you are not. If you're waiting for a permission slip, this is it. Not to destroy your life for the sake of starting over, but to refine it until it reflects your real signal. This might mean changing how you show up in conversations. It might mean shifting how you schedule your days. It might mean saying no to something that technically "works" but doesn't resonate. It might mean saying yes to something that scares you because it's finally aligned.

There is no formula. But there is one consistent requirement: you must be willing to choose what is true, even when it costs you the comfort of the familiar. That is the moment rebellion becomes a portal. It's not just about what you leave behind. It's about what you open up to. The level of reality that only becomes accessible when you are no longer playing by rules that were designed to keep you quiet, small, or useful to someone else's system. Rebellion is not the end of your obedience. It is the beginning of your authorship. The moment you stop waiting to be allowed and begin deciding to be. Not just once, but over and over, until your life no longer resembles anything that was built through fear. That is not resistance. That is reverence.

Chapter 12. Living Buried No More

The Integration Formula: Identity + Ritual + Field

Abundance is not just something you call in. It's something you sustain. And that sustaining force isn't random. It's not about waiting to feel "high vibe," or about catching momentum and hoping it lasts. It's about integration. Daily, cellular, atmospheric integration.

That's why this isn't a mindset trick. It's a framework. One you can return to again and again. When things wobble. When you expand and your nervous system starts resisting. When you begin to receive, and then start to sabotage. When old loops creep back in. When your outer world starts to reflect a signal you thought you had outgrown.

The Integration Formula is made of three core components: Identity, Ritual, and Field. Each one supports the others. And when they're all aligned, abundance is not just a temporary state. It becomes an embodied baseline. Something your system naturally holds without constant force, hustle, or control.

Let's break this down in a way that makes it immediately usable.

1. Identity: The Internal Anchor

Everything you receive, allow, or block is filtered through the identity you believe yourself to be. Identity is not just how you think of yourself. It's how your system is *coded* to operate. It includes your emotional home, your perceived limits, and your subconscious expectations about what is possible, safe, or even *yours to have*.

An identity that is unconsciously wired for scarcity will unconsciously leak, reject, or repel abundance, no matter how many affirmations you repeat. On the other hand, when your identity is stabilized around overflow, it becomes too costly to keep living in lack. The nervous system starts to treat poverty, struggle, and contraction as foreign, instead of familiar. That's when expansion becomes the new home.

So the question becomes: who are you *being* as you create, relate, spend, receive, and rest?

Identity work is not about perfection. It's about congruence. Not trying to *fake* abundance, but aligning how you speak, behave, and choose with the frequency of someone who already *has permission* to receive. It means asking, consistently, "What would I choose right now if I knew I was already safe, already supported, already chosen?"

If you find that your identity flips between lack and overflow depending on your bank account, your client schedule, or someone else's response, that doesn't mean you've failed. It just means the code needs reinforcing. And that's where ritual comes in.

2. Ritual: The Behavioral Code

You cannot stabilize an expanded identity without tangible reinforcement. That's what ritual is for. Rituals are not routines. They are *coded behaviors* that tell your system what to expect and what to normalize.

A ritual, in this formula, is any recurring act that tells your body, "This is who we are now." It can be subtle. It can be private. It doesn't need to be mystical. But it *does* need to be consistent and intentional. A daily walk at a certain hour to signal spaciousness. A specific way you open your laptop to anchor presence before work. A weekly review that celebrates receipts, even before money arrives. A closing gesture at the end of each day that says, "We did enough."

These acts create coherence between the story you're claiming and the signals you're living. They prevent backsliding into self-doubt because they anchor your identity into physical space and time. They remind your subconscious, "This is no longer a dream. This is now."

The third component, the field, is often the most overlooked. While identity and ritual are internal and behavioral, the field is relational and environmental. It's the energetic ecosystem you are steeped in, whether you're aware of it or not. And that field is always shaping your frequency, reinforcing or diluting your signals.

The field includes your home, your workspace, your technology, your conversations, your money containers, and even your digital environment. Every item, every relationship, every channel holds a signal. And when those signals contradict the identity and rituals you're working to stabilize, they begin to create friction, noise, or distortion.

You might be showing up with grounded certainty in your daily rituals, but if you're surrounded by people constantly speaking scarcity, or environments that trigger contraction, your field becomes mismatched.

That mismatch doesn't just make it harder to maintain momentum. It slowly starts to erode the integrity of the identity you're anchoring.

To refine the field, you don't need to escape your life or remove everyone who's not "on your level." What matters more is how intentional you are with energetic exposure. What do you let influence you? Where does your attention land during the most impressionable parts of your day — waking, resting, transitions, creative openings? Who do you let speak into your process, and what tone do those voices carry?

The goal isn't to curate some perfect bubble. It's to shape your field to reflect the frequency you're holding, so it feeds instead of drains you. That might mean restructuring your calendar to include space between external demands. It might mean creating digital boundaries — what you check first, who you reply to, what you consume. It might mean rearranging your physical space to mirror the version of you who already feels resourced, received, and real.

A coherent field doesn't just support you. It confirms you. It helps your nervous system feel safe in the new identity because everything around you begins to validate the shift. That validation is not about ego. It's about stability. The more evidence your system receives that the new signal is safe, the easier it is to stay there without self-sabotage.

Now, these three components — identity, ritual, and field — are not linear steps. They work together in a cycle. You anchor the identity, reinforce it through ritual, and protect it through field curation. As your abundance expands, you revisit all three and adjust. New levels of receiving require new versions of all three. Not because you were wrong before, but because each expansion demands a deeper alignment.

When you find yourself slipping into doubt, depletion, or disconnection, instead of spiraling, use this formula as a check-in. Ask:

Is my identity still coded for this level?

Are my rituals reinforcing what I'm claiming?

Is my field congruent with what I say I want?

Often, the most subtle misalignment in just one of these areas is enough to cancel out your signal. But that's not a failure. It's data. It's feedback from your system, showing you exactly where to recalibrate.

The power of this formula is not just in manifestation. It's in maintenance. In integration. In learning to live at the frequency you used to chase. When these three pieces click into place, you stop reaching. You stop managing. You stop oscillating between hope and disappointment. Instead, you create from a place of already. You move from a baseline of enoughness. You become the stable point from which abundance naturally flows.

This is what makes overflow sustainable. Not the spikes, not the wins, not the high moments of magic — but the grounded system that holds them, again and again, because it's been built to. Because you've become the one who knows how.

No More Loops: Spotting and Disrupting the Slide Back

Regression doesn't always show up as dramatic collapse. It's often subtle. A few skipped rituals. A quiet re-emergence of old thoughts. A familiar fatigue you explain away. And before you realize it, you're back inside the old loop — not because your work failed, but because the system you changed hasn't yet become your default.

When you shift your frequency, you create a rupture in the old pattern. But unless that new frequency is consistently reinforced, the body-mind system will try to conserve energy by reverting to what it knows. The slide back is not a flaw in your transformation. It's a normal part of integration. What matters is whether you catch it early or only recognize it once it has already pulled you under.

The key to staying out of the loop is not perfection. It's pattern recognition. And the sooner you notice the signature of regression, the easier it is to disrupt it before it regains momentum.

Regression almost always begins with a frequency drop before it becomes visible. This drop can be felt as a contraction — a heaviness behind your eyes, a weight in your chest, a sense of background noise getting louder. It might disguise itself as "tired," "busy," or "not in the mood," but the deeper truth is that your energetic system is starting to withdraw.

One of the clearest signs is the loss of intentionality. You stop choosing your direction, and start reacting. You check your phone before you check in with yourself. You default to other people's rhythms instead of holding your own. You shift from being the transmitter of your frequency to absorbing what's around you. These small compromises seem harmless in the moment, but they add up quickly. And each one weakens the signal you worked so hard to calibrate.

Another sign is emotional fragmentation. You might feel "off" without knowing why. Old stories start to sound reasonable again. You rationalize scarcity. You justify shrinking. You abandon the boundaries that once felt non-negotiable. What's happening here is not a loss of clarity, but a slow erosion of coherence. The parts of you that used to align with the new reality are being pulled apart by competing inputs, often beneath your awareness.

To break this cycle, you need a clear and embodied protocol for disruption — something that does not rely on willpower, but on awareness and energetic reset. Willpower is too unreliable in a state of contraction. But presence, when activated properly, can cut through the fog like a blade.

The Disruption Sequence

This protocol isn't about fixing anything. It's about noticing early, interrupting the slide, and reactivating your signal. Each step is meant to be felt, not rushed.

1. **Recognize the distortion signal.** This means becoming sensitive to the earliest indicators of misalignment — before it becomes behavior. You'll start to notice a texture in your body: shallow breathing, tension around the jaw, sudden urgency. Stop immediately when you feel it. Don't negotiate. Don't postpone. Awareness is the intervention.
2. **Pause the external input.** This is non-negotiable. Turn off notifications. Step away from the screen. Interrupt the loop of absorption. If you're listening to others' energy more than your own, you're not in the seat of creation anymore. Come back.
3. **Drop into sensation, not story.** Most people try to fix regression by thinking their way out. That keeps the loop alive. Instead, get into the body. Find where the frequency lives. Feel it without fixing it. Let it speak. You'll be surprised how quickly energy shifts when it is acknowledged instead of avoided.

Let the sensation open without needing to label it. Is it fear? Shame? Doubt? Maybe. But what matters more is the frequency it's carrying. Stay with it just long enough to feel it without collapsing into it. Your presence is what transmutes it. Not logic. Not solving. Just pure awareness.

Once you've anchored your attention back in the body, the signal becomes available again. The loop loses its charge when you stop running from it. And now, from that cleared space, you have access to choice again.

The next move is a pattern break. Something that disrupts the predictable neural loop that was about to tighten. It doesn't have to be elaborate. Stand up. Splash cold water on your face. Open a window. Breathe. Play a track that reminds you of who you are. The nervous system responds powerfully to interruption when it's paired with presence. That one shift can halt an entire cascade.

Now it's time to reprogram the moment. Ask yourself a simple question: *What was I about to do or decide from a compromised frequency?* You might have been about to say yes to something that drains you. Or scroll through content that derails you. Or entertain an old belief dressed in new clothes. Once you name the move you were about to make, you have reclaimed the steering wheel. Now reverse it.

Instead of playing out the loop, take an aligned micro-action. Something small, but energetically clean. If you were about to contract, expand. If you were about to postpone, commit. If you were about to stay silent, speak. The action doesn't need to be dramatic. What matters is that it's initiated from the frequency of your chosen identity, not from the echo of the old self.

This isn't about being on high alert all the time. It's about having a reflex for restoration. Once your system learns that you will catch yourself, that you will return without punishment or panic, the need for regression weakens. You teach your field that coherence is your new baseline, not a high you chase but a ground you return to. Over time, these reactivations become automatic. You'll sense a loop before it forms, and redirect it without needing to fall inside it first.

The power of this practice is not just in avoiding setbacks. It's in developing a new kind of self-trust. A trust rooted not in control, but in response. You start to trust that no matter how the energy shifts, you will know what to do with it. And that trust becomes the foundation of your forward momentum. There will always be friction at the edges of expansion. But now you know what to do with it. You don't need to fear the slide, because you no longer leave it undetected. You don't need to avoid contraction, because you've learned how to walk through it without losing yourself.

The loop isn't the problem. The real danger is when you forget you have the authority to exit it. This chapter isn't about prevention. It's about remembering. Remembering that every pattern that once ran your life can be paused, interrupted, and rewritten in real time. That you can feel the pull and still say no. That you can catch yourself mid-contraction and shift your signal before it becomes your story.

You are not the pattern. You are the one who decides whether it plays. And now you have a protocol that makes that choice real.

Let this be your new agreement with yourself: no more loops. Not because they no longer try to form, but because you no longer feed them. You return to signal. You return to self. You return to power. Again and again, until return becomes embodiment.

What It Means to Become a Living Portal of Wealth

There is a moment, often quiet and without fanfare, when wealth stops being something you chase and starts becoming something you carry. You are no longer reaching for the codes. You are the code. This shift is not marked by the size of your bank account or the number of manifestations you've ticked off a list. It is marked by the way your field speaks before your mouth does. The way rooms shift before you enter. The way life begins to arrange itself around your internal certainty.

To become a living portal of wealth means you no longer relate to abundance as something external. It is not something to attract, manage, or protect. It is not a prize for good behavior or an outcome of perfect strategy. It is your native frequency. The foundation of your decisions. The default posture of your nervous system.

This doesn't mean you're always calm, always clear, always high-vibrational. It means that even when turbulence comes, you no longer collapse. You hold. You stabilize. You anchor wealth not because you're always in a perfect emotional state, but because your identity is no longer negotiable. You know who you are. You know what you carry. And life responds to that.

A living portal does not hoard, clutch, or rush. There is no panic in her signal. She doesn't strive to prove her worth or barter with the universe for scraps of validation. She walks with the knowing that she *is* the opening through which wealth arrives. And not just wealth in numbers. Wealth in time, in space, in beauty, in intimacy, in expression. She knows that what flows to her is a match for what flows through her.

This way of being is not performative. It isn't about aesthetic rituals or curated words. It's in the tone of your voice when you say yes. In the quiet confidence of your no. In the way you make decisions from overflow instead of lack. It's how you give without depletion, receive without guilt, and build without burnout.

People feel it. They may not know what it is, but they sense the difference. There's a frequency to someone who no longer waits for permission. Whose worth is not on trial. Whose signal does not flicker based on feedback, algorithms, or applause. That person carries wealth in their field. Not because of what they've acquired, but because of what they've remembered.

There will be times when the old identity knocks again. Times when you are tempted to shrink, to compromise, to delay. That's part of it. But the portal version of you no longer treats those moments as evidence. You recognize them for what they are: echoes. Faint and fading. Not who you are now.

To embody living abundance is to walk the world as a transmitter, not a seeker. You become the source, not just the recipient. You no longer wait to feel abundant in order to move. You move because you *are* abundance in motion. This is not a mindset. It is a calibration. A cellular shift. A coded stance.

Even the way you rest changes. Rest is no longer collapse or escape. It becomes part of your magnetism. Stillness becomes a power source. Silence becomes a signal. You are no longer running to keep up with the life you want. You are rooted in it. And from that rootedness, everything accelerates. Your presence is no longer just personal. It becomes a fieldwide invitation. Others feel safer around you. Braver. More open. Your frequency becomes an activation in itself. You walk into a space and remind others what is possible. You speak, and something in them remembers their own signal. Not because you're trying to teach. But because you *are*.

There is a gravity to someone who no longer confuses chaos with aliveness. You are no longer seduced by noise, urgency, or lack masquerading as opportunity. You know what is real because you feel it in your body. You feel when something expands your field or contracts it. You are no longer available for the frantic chase, for the self-abandonment hidden in the pursuit of "more." Your nervous system no longer mistakes survival for success.

The portal version of you is not just energetically clean. She is structurally aligned. Your space reflects the signal. Your habits, your timing, your relationships, your containers all point to the same truth: you are abundance. You do not leak it through self-neglect, people-pleasing, or overstaying where your value is unseen. Every part of your life becomes a declaration of what you're willing to hold.

This identity holds paradox with ease. It knows when to push and when to pause. It can move with fire and sit in silence. It does not rush integration. It does not fear contrast. It knows that refinement is not regression, and solitude is not abandonment. You become sovereign in your calibration, which means no one else dictates your pace, your worth, or your direction. You are not above learning, but you are no longer in the posture of proving. You also begin to sense the deeper intelligence of desire. You stop treating your longings as indulgent or excessive. You see them as maps. Desires that persist are not there to torment you. They are frequencies that belong to you, echoing forward in time, waiting for you to catch up. When you embody the portal, you no longer shrink your capacity to match your current circumstances. You stretch your field to receive what's already yours in the unseen.

This is why people start to say things like, "You've changed" or "You're glowing" or "You feel different." They're picking up on something that has nothing to do with surface. They are sensing your field has organized. That you are no longer broadcasting mixed signals. That your signal is clear, unbothered, untangled. They can't explain it, but they feel it.

And the truth is, you feel it too. You move through the world with less static. Less friction. Less doubt. You don't need to know the "how" anymore because you've met the "who." You are the version of you that doesn't sabotage her clarity or outsource her power. You have become the space where miracles normalize, not because you chase magic, but because you've become a stable container for it.

In this identity, there is no more arguing with reality. You don't negotiate with fear. You don't explain your abundance. You don't delay what you know is yours. You simply continue. Continue walking. Continue anchoring. Continue expanding. Not from pressure, but from devotion. You understand now that the portal doesn't perform. It doesn't announce. It transmits. Silently. Powerfully. Consistently.

Eventually, the world catches up. The money follows. The timing aligns. The rooms shift. Not because you forced it, but because you stopped leaking signal. You stopped wavering. You became the axis, and reality organized around you.

This is not a role you play. It's not a performance you maintain. It's a frequency you embody until it becomes who you are. A portal of wealth is not someone who has it all. It's someone who *is* it all. And in that embodiment, there is nothing left to chase.

There is only receiving. Only refining. Only remembering. Over and over again. Until the life around you begins to look and feel like the truth you've always carried inside.

Last Words

If you made it here, something has already shifted.
Not just in your thoughts, but in your field.
You've walked through layers most people avoid.
You've touched the hidden architecture of what was never yours.
And piece by piece, you've started to return to yourself.
This book wasn't meant to *teach* you.
It was meant to *remember* you.
You don't have to read more.
You don't have to fix anything.
You don't have to force what's already in motion.
Just keep listening.
Keep choosing what aligns.
Keep refusing to shrink.
You are not the one who waits.
You are not the one who chases.
You are the one who receives.
Thank you for trusting this process.
Thank you for trusting *yourself*.
This is not the end.
This is what it feels like to begin again — inside the truth.

www.ingramcontent.com/pod-product-compliance
Lightning Source LLC
Chambersburg PA
CBHW060348090426
42734CB00011B/2071